AFRIKAN-CENTERED CONSCIOUSNESS *VERSUS* THE NEW WORLD ORDER

Garveyism in the Age of Globalism

AMOS N. WILSON

ISBN 13: 978-1-879164-09-3
Reprinted 2024
9 8 7 6 5 4

Executive Editor: Sababu N. Plata
Assistant Editor: Adisa Makalani
Copy Editor: Raven Rowe
Graphics Illustrator: Joseph Gillians

Library of Congress Cataloging-in-Publication Data

Wilson, Amos N., author.
Afrikan-centered consciousness versus the new world order : Garveyism in the age of globalism / Amos N. Wilson.
pages cm
ISBN 978-1-879164-09-3 (alk. paper) —ISBN 1-879164-09-4
1. Garvey, Marcus, 1887-1940—Influence.
2. African Americans—Race identity. 3. Blacks—Race identity.
4. Black nationalism. 5. African diaspora. I. Title.
E185.97.G3W55 2015
305.896'073—dc23
2015026717

AFRIKAN WORLD INFOSYSTEMS
743 Rogers Avenue, Suite 6/3L
Brooklyn, New York 11226
E-mail: Afrikanworld@aol.com
Web page: www.Afrikanworldinfosystems.co

Printed in Canada

AFRIKAN-CENTERED CONSCIOUSNESS *VERSUS* THE NEW WORLD ORDER

Garveyism in the Age of Globalism

AMOS N. WILSON

New York
Afrikan World InfoSystems

Also by Amos N. Wilson

Black-on-Black Violence: *The Psychodynamics of Black Self-Annihilation in Service of White Domination*

The Developmental Psychology of the Black Child

Issues of Manhood in Black and White: *An Incisive Look into Masculinity and the Societal Definition of Afrikan Man* (INCLUDES Understanding Black Adolescent Male Violence)

The Falsification of Afrikan Consciousness: *Eurocentric History, Psychiatry and the Politics of White Supremacy*

Afrikan-centered Consciousness Versus the New World Order: *Garveyism in the Age of Globalism*

Blueprint For Black Power: *A Moral, Political and Economic Imperative for the Twenty-First Century*

The Psychology of Self-Hatred and Self-Defeat: *Towards a Reclamation of the Afrikan Mind*

Dedication

To the memory of Samori Marksman,
Roy Canton and Paul Buckmire

Acknowledgments

Though the preparation of a book is a highly social process, it takes place in considerable isolation. Throughout its gestation, the unfurling of life's chances and challenges stop not for a moment. This effort squarely fits into that mold.

The closing of 1998 and the opening months of 1999 were fraught with heart-wrenching agony and shock. Just as we celebrated the publishing of *Blueprint for Black Power*, the ancestors called HOME freedom fighters John Henrik Clarke, Roy Canton, Kwame Ture and Samori Marksman. Personal old friend Paul "Bucky" Buckmire and our family childhood friend, a young Elvin Roach, both died suddenly. Bucky would often sit afternoons and have grand conversations of further endeavors in Pan-Afrikan service. Vin, a true friend, little known except in the immediate circle of Arima, was like the other distinguished warriors, ever-present in all manner of need. Indeed, they graced us with meritorious service. May they RISE LIKE RA!

We mourned, venerated their life expressions, and then, it was time to reassume revolution's challenges.

And thus this long-mused publication was elevated to the fore. We rallied veterans and new recruits alike to blast into being—in record time—these most compelling of Dr. Wilson's discourses. Embrace this the fruit of the vineyard.

We first give thanks to the ancestors in whose path we follow, being ever vigilant in the struggle for true dignity and liberation.

Kudos to staff members Lolita Lopez, Raven Rowe and Adisa Makalani for diligently editing, proofing, and spiritedly commenting on the manuscript. Of additional note is the transcribing, cross referencing and prompt communications of Brother Adisa.

Joseph Gillians answered the call to pen the overview of Marcus Garvey. He served to lay the historical and political context and tone, and thus fortified the subsequent presentations of Brother Amos; this in addition to being graphic illustrator and researcher. We salute these efforts.

Commendations to Nzinga Nosakhene for her appraisal, candid critique and feisty defense of her opinions.

To Utrice Leid and other staffers at WBAI, for mandating the prompt completion of this work we utter the Jamaican refrain "nuff respect! "

To those whose contributions were beyond the call of friendship, the many associates, admirers and disseminators who undergird our work, we extend sincerest gratitude for your support over the years.

Lastly, we exalt the clairvoyance of *our* brother, Amos N. Wilson. Know that we stand resolute in the struggle to bring into being a new world order!

Contents

With best wishes
you obedient servant
Marcus Garvey

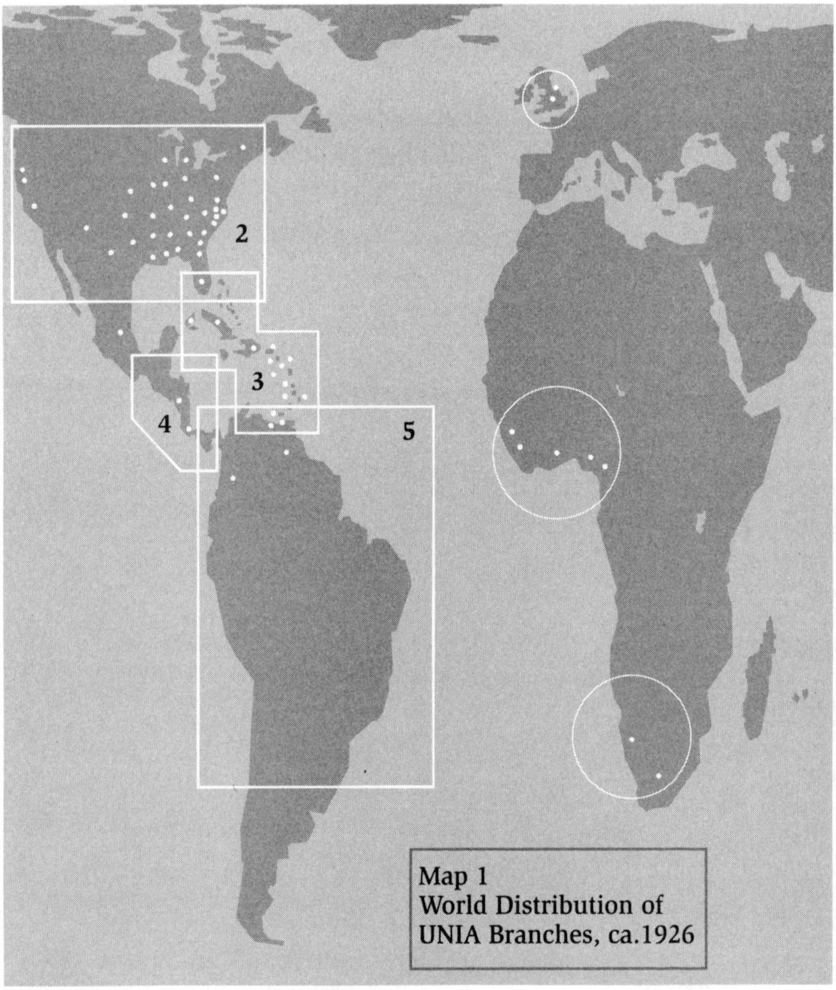

Countries not shown on maps

	Number of Branches
Australia	1
England	2
Gold Coast (Ghana)	2
Liberia	2
Nigeria	1
Sierra Leone	3
South Afrika	8
South West Afrika (Namibia)	2
Wales	2

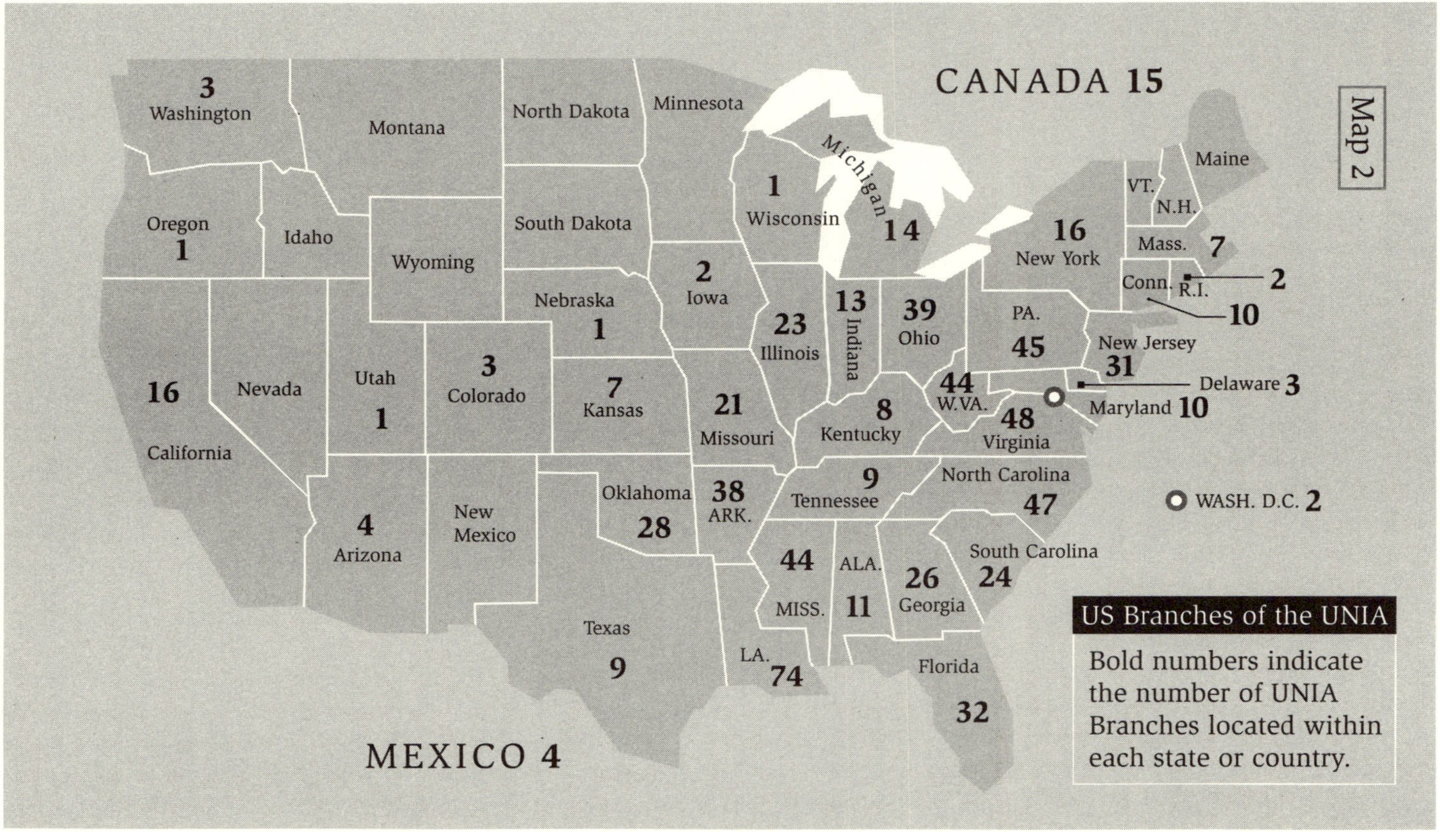

Map 2

US Branches of the UNIA

Bold numbers indicate the number of UNIA Branches located within each state or country.

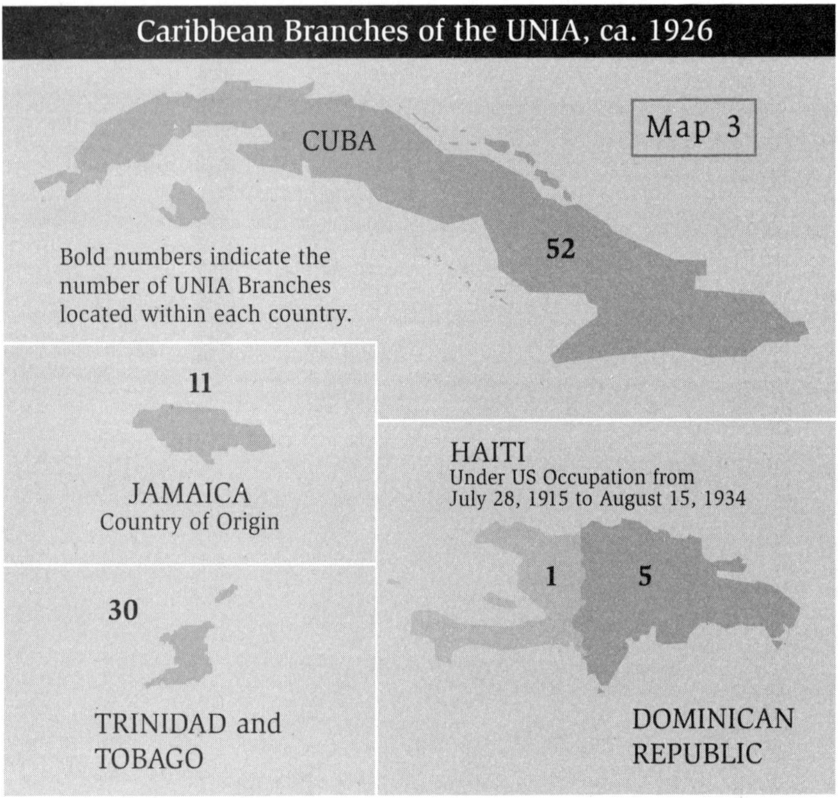

Islands not shown on map	Number of Branches
Antigua	**1**
Bahamas	**2**
Barbados	**4**
Bermuda	**1**
Dominica	**1**
Grenada	**1**
Puerto Rico	**1**
St. Kitts-Nevis-Anguilla	**1**
St. Lucia	**1**
St. Thomas	**1**
St. Vincent	**1**

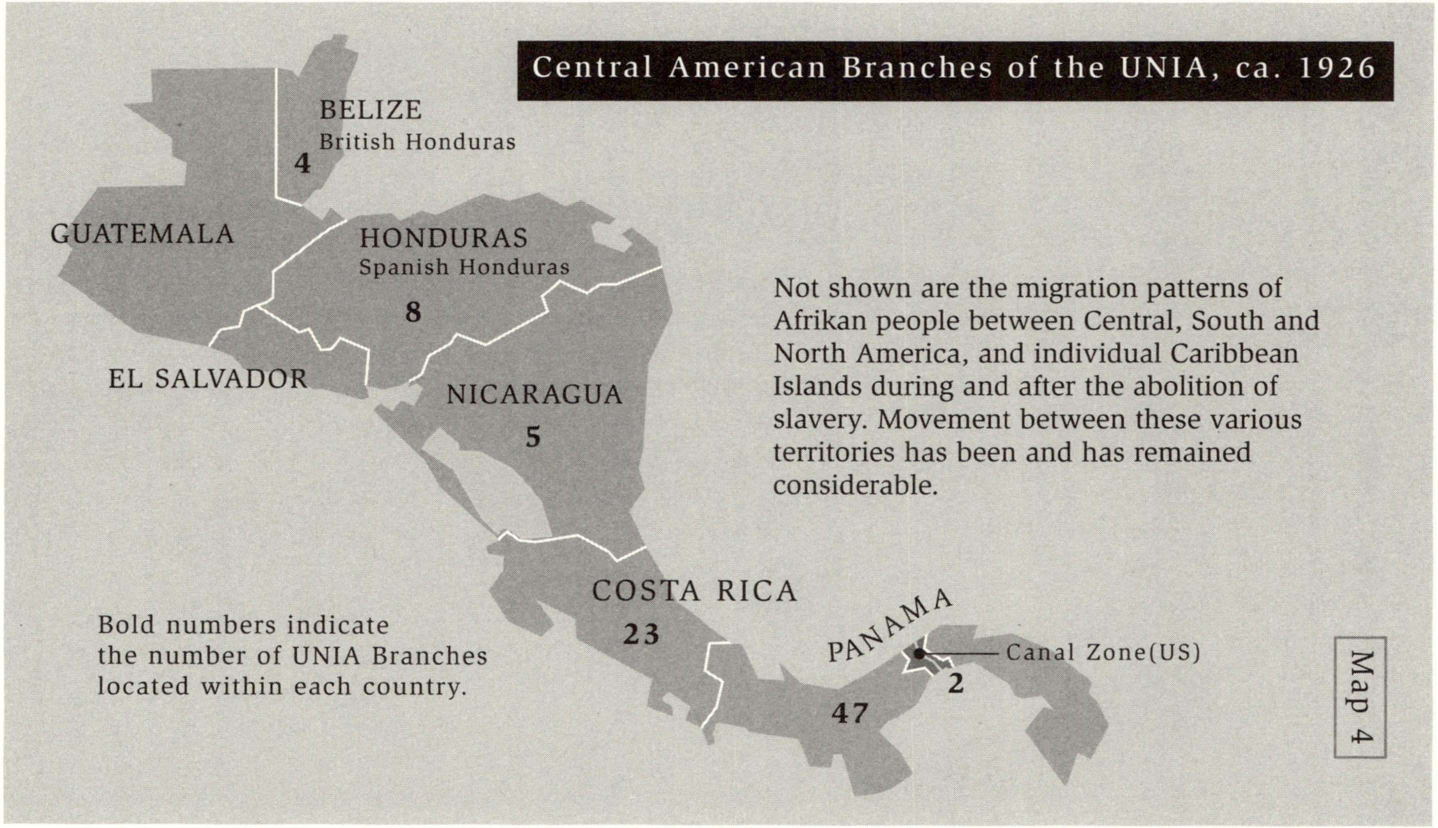
Central American Branches of the UNIA, ca. 1926
BELIZE
British Honduras
4
GUATEMALA
HONDURAS
Spanish Honduras
8
EL SALVADOR
NICARAGUA
5
COSTA RICA
23
PANAMA
47
Canal Zone(US)
2
Not shown are the migration patterns of Afrikan people between Central, South and North America, and individual Caribbean Islands during and after the abolition of slavery. Movement between these various territories has been and has remained considerable.
Bold numbers indicate the number of UNIA Branches located within each country.
Map 4

South American Branches of the UNIA, ca. 1926

A Short List of the Ideological and Pan-Afrikan Predecessors and Descendents of the UNIA

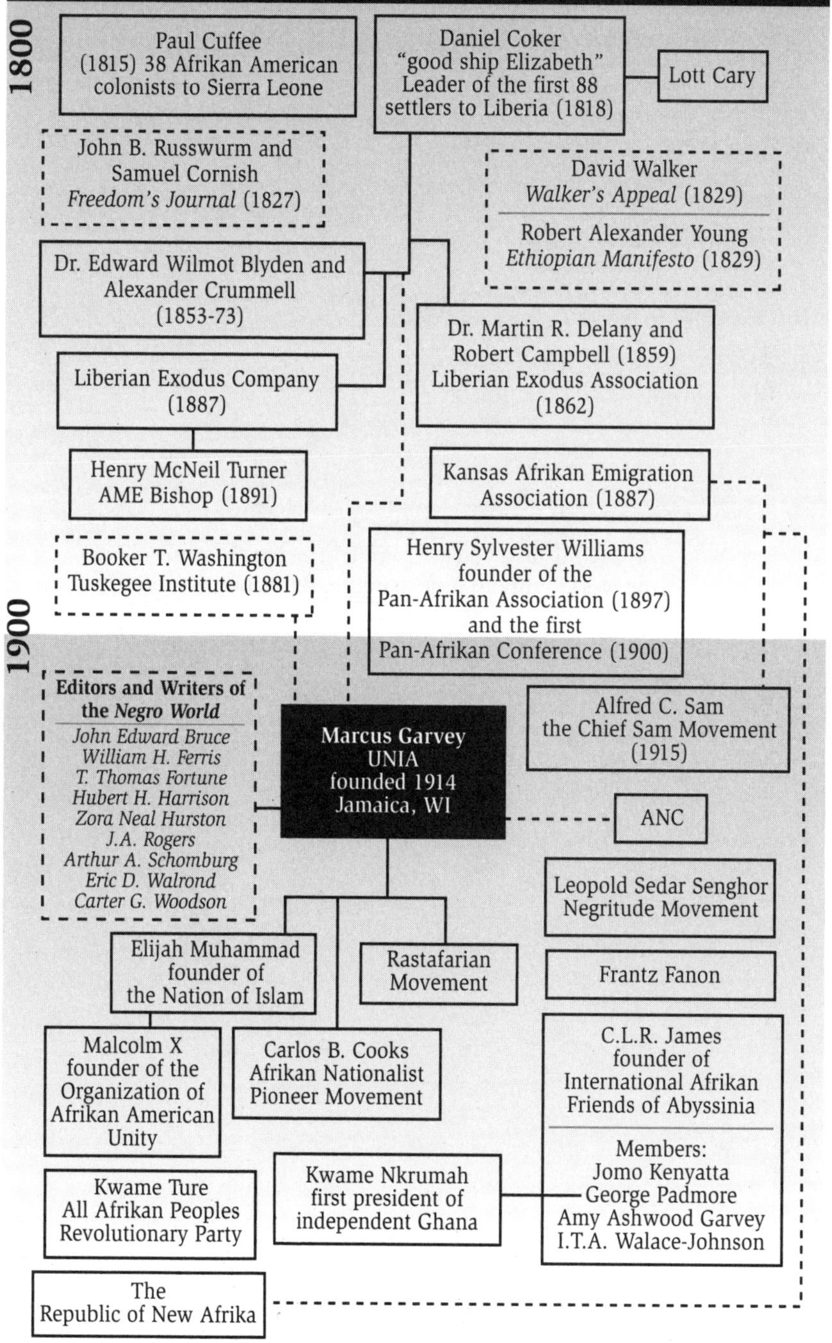

My mistake you ask? Well, I tried to change
the world without first changing the minds of men.

–Marcus Garvey

Historical Overview of Marcus Garvey

We at Afrikan World InFoSystems reprint here only a segment of the letter from the Honorable Marcus Garvey titled "First Message to the Negroes of the World from Atlanta Prison" dated February 10, 1925, so that the reader may begin to more fully grasp the spirit of the man who inspired our beloved brother, Dr. Amos N. Wilson

. . . All I have I have given to you. I have sacrificed my home and my loving wife for you. I entrust her to your charge, to protect and defend her in my absence. She is the bravest little woman I know. She has suffered and sacrificed with me for you; therefore, please do not desert her in this dismal hour, when she stands alone. I have left her penniless and helpless to face the world, because I gave all, but her courage is great, and I know she will hold up for you and me.

After my enemies are satisfied, in life or death I shall come back to you to serve even as I have served before. In life I shall be the same; in death I shall be a terror to the foes of Negro liberty. If death has power, then count on me in death to be the real Marcus Garvey I would like to be. I may come in an earthquake, or a cyclone, or plague, or pestilence, or as God would have me, then be assured that I shall never desert you and make your enemies triumph over you. Would I not go to hell a million times for you? Would I not like Macbeth's ghost, walk the earth forever for you? Would I not lose the whole world and eternity for you? Would I not cry forever before the footstool of the Lord Omnipotent for you? Would I not die a million deaths for you? Then, why be sad? Cheer up, and be assured that if it takes a million years the sins of our enemies shall visit the millionth generation of those that hinder and oppress us.

Remember that I have sworn by you and my God to serve to the end of all time, the wreck of matter and the crash of worlds. The enemies think I am defeated. Did the Germans defeat the French in 1870? Did Napoleon really conquer Europe? If so, then I am defeated, but I tell you the world shall hear from my principles, even two thousand years hence. I am willing to wait on time for my satisfaction and the retribution of my enemies. Observe my enemies and their children and posterity, and one day you shall see retribution settling around them.

If I die in Atlanta my work shall live, in the physical or spiritual to see the day of Africa's glory. When I am dead wrap the mantle of the Red, Black and Green around me, for in the new life I shall rise with God's grace and blessing to lead the millions up the heights of triumph with the colors that you all know. Look for me in the whirlwind or the storm, look for me all around you, for, with God's grace I shall come and bring with me countless millions of Black slaves who have died in America and the West Indies and the millions in Africa to aid you in the fight for Liberty, Freedom and Life.

The civilization of today is gone drunk and crazy with its power and by such it seeks through injustice, fraud and lies to crush the unfortunate. But if I am apparently crushed by the system of influence and misdirected power, my cause shall rise again to plague the conscience of the corrupt. For I am satisfied, and for you, I repeat, I am glad to suffer and even die. Again I say, cheer up, for better days are ahead. I shall write the history that will inspire the millions that are coming and leave the posterity of our enemies to reckon with the hosts for the deeds of their fathers.

With God's dearest blessings, I leave you for awhile.

– MARCUS GARVEY

Garvey's statement, "All I have I have given to you," is on his part an understatement. If humanly possible, he gave immeasurably more. From the age of twenty he was already at work organizing on behalf of his fellow countrymen and writing in glaring detail of the brutality and injustice that defined their wretched condition. On this he never compromised, and it cost him dearly in both health and worldly possessions.

It all began amid the sweet rolling hills and languid breezes of his native Jamaica. The arresting beauty of the island belied its long bloody history of war, brute slavery, genocide, ecocide, pestilence and suffering of its contemporary Black inhabitants. On August 17, 1887 in St Ann's Bay, Marcus Mosiah Garvey was born into this world of stark contradictions. Of the eleven children born to Sarah and Marcus Garvey, young Marcus and his older sister Indiana were the only siblings to live past childhood.

The elder Marcus was a proud descendant of the Maroons, a community of Afrikan runaways who wrenched their freedom from the British by force of arms. A master stone mason reputedly as strong as an ox, he was a passionate lover of books of which he owned a considerable number. The possession of a library distinguished him in a community of small-scale peasant farmers of simple means and modest ways. His wife, Sarah, was said to have been extraordinarily beautiful; a wonderfully black woman with luxuriously smooth skin. She was the business anchor of the family. Along with one of her brothers, she owned a parcel of land on which pimentos and citrus fruits were grown for market. She also baked pastries made from coconut and guava and sold the popular delights at a decent profit. From his mother's efforts "to put a little something aside," Marcus learned industry. From his father, the younger Marcus inherited physical strength, initiative and love of reading.

Family hardship forced Marcus to leave school at age fourteen to be apprenticed out to his godfather to learn the trade of printing. In 1903 when Marcus was sixteen, a hurricane wiped out the crops (yam, cocoa, cassava and fruit trees) causing the family further economic hardship. Marcus decided to move to Kingston and try his luck there, promising his mother that as soon as things improved he would send for the family. With the assistance of a maternal uncle, Marcus secured a job at Benjamin's Printery, at which he became the youngest foreman in the history of the trade – at just 18 years old. This was at a time when white laborers from abroad were being hired to fill managerial positions. He saved his money and was able to keep his promise to his mother. The good times were short-lived, however. In 1907 an earthquake and resulting fire flattened much of Kingston, killing 800 people. Although the British government extended the colony a loan to rebuild, it did little to help the sagging economy. Wages were low, prices high, commodities scarce or, in some cases, nonexistent. Workers all over the island were in desperate straits.

The first trade union to be formed on the island, the Printers' Union, struck, demanding higher wages. In sympathy, Garvey, a foreman, joined his fellow workers on the picket line even though he had been individually offered a raise. American printers' unions sent monetary assistance to the strikers through the difficult times, but the treasurer of the Jamaican union absconded with the money. The men became demoralized and the bond between them began to unravel. Despite assurances to the contrary, his support for the strike cost Garvey his job, but he was able to find employment again, this time at the Government Printing Office.

Kingston was where Garvey's political views began to take shape. Unlike the countryside where he spent an unhurried childhood within a close-knit community of small-scale peasant farmers, the city offered the opportunity to engage people from diverse backgrounds, occupations, and experiences. He got involved in the city's intellectual life, frequenting all places known for debates – including barbershops and park bench gatherings. For weeks he quietly observed, then after a shy approach joined in. His inexperience got him in trouble; ideas which he felt were well thought out were torn to shreds. He smarted at the ridicule, "Country boy shut up!" The trailing laughter hurt Garvey deeply and he vowed never again. He was determined to become learned. Since there were no elocution lessons offered in the public theaters or elsewhere on the island, he visited churches, studied the delivery of preachers, their sermons and manner of deportment. His pursuit of the art of public speaking led him to take lessons from a man who was initially his role model, then mentor, Dr. J. Robert Love, an English-educated Black physician from Nassau, Bahamas, who settled in Jamaica and published a newspaper called *The Advocate.* He spent his entire career and economic resources fighting to better health conditions for the island's suffering poor. With time and practice Marcus became accomplished. This was no isolated undertaking for as he sharpened his skill he taught others. Soon he was conducting elocution contests with prizes donated by Kingston's prominent citizens.

Garvey's budding activities brought him in contact with the National Club, Jamaica's first political club, organized by lawyer and council member Sandy Cox. The group was formed to fight the harsh excesses of British colonialism on the island. Garvey was made assistant secretary and helped to publish the Club's pamphlet, *Our Own*, fortnightly.

Organizing for social uplift is hard, demanding, full-time work, as anyone who has ever embarked upon knows. It became clear to the young Marcus that this part-time effort would not suffice. He decided after careful thought to quit his job at the Government Printing Office. This bold step gave birth to another Garvey-initiated paper, *The Watchman*. The year was 1910; Garvey, a mere 23 years old. The economic rigors of running and organizing the newspaper soon drained his resources. Penniless and without a means to a livelihood he left the security of his island home for Costa Rica where the United Fruit Company [now multinationals Chiquita and Dole] was clearing ground and planting bananas with the use of cheap labor from the colonized lands of the Caribbean, Central and South America. There, a maternal uncle got him a job as a timekeeper, and thus began another mean lesson in the condition of Blacks. The work environment was horrid – deadly! Snake- and disease-infested swamps were only the crust of the misery. The roads to and from nearby towns were deathtraps – literally killing fields – where bandits regularly preyed upon the workers, robbed and often hacked them to death with machetes. Black bodies festered in the undergrowth and bloated till white in the country's rivers. Repulsed, Garvey resigned and headed straight for coastal city Port Limón. Upon his arrival he found further to his dismay that what the bandits didn't get from the workers was often ripped off by the unregulated banks. He protested, pressing upon the ear of the British Consul to help their Black "subjects." "If they don't like conditions here, they can leave," was the reply. The brutal lesson on the value of Black life sunk in – deep.

The consul's arrogance and nonchalance spurred Garvey to take matters into his own hands. He found work on the docks as a laborer, scraped together what resources he could and published *La Nación*, a newspaper to unite his fellow Blacks that they might press for better working conditions and higher pay. He simultaneously harried the British Consul on behalf of fellow Blacks. However, worker disunity — fear laced with political apathy — soon put the fledgling newspaper out of business. For all his efforts Garvey was arrested for agitating the workers. To avoid the wrath of the authorities he fled Costa Rica for Bocas del Toro in the Republic of Panama, that neck of land between the vast Atlantic and Pacific oceans. It widened Marcus' panorama of Afrikan suffering like a descent into Dante's *Inferno*: "Abandon all hope all ye that enter here."

In 1911, when Garvey arrived, the Panama Canal, "The Big Ditch", was still three years from completion. Work on the enormous earthwork was started by a French company in 1882, the same company that completed the Suez Canal in 1869. Under the French the project failed abysmally. Mismanagement, theft, inhospitable terrain and epidemics of tropical diseases that killed 22,000 men, predominantly low-paid Afrikan Caribbean labor, drove the project to a halt and the company into bankruptcy in 1889. In 1903 the United States paid France $40 million for the property, but work on the Canal did not resume in earnest until 1907. Although much had been done to eradicate disease,[1] and sanitation improved, Garvey was appalled by the squalid living conditions of Black labor: many with families occupied clapboard shacks with little or no protection from the dreaded mosquito. American knowhow was accompa-

1. The last recorded death from yellow fever in Panama occurred in 1907, but malaria continued to take its toll in human lives.

nied by American racism. Jim Crow was the order of the day. Back-breaking conditions, worker abuse and salary disparity were rampant. Blacks were paid in silver coins, Whites in gold!

Garvey protested these horrors and once again his urgent pleas on behalf of his fellow Blacks were met with disdain. He started *La Prensa*, a news vehicle to publicize their plight. It did little good. His agitation met a brick wall. He left Panama and for the next year descended further into the abyss: Ecuador, Nicaragua, Honduras, Columbia and Venezuela all offered up their torrid versions of Black suffering. Sickened by the experience and ill with fever, Garvey returned home to Jamaica with the thought that he might get results from the home government. The disdainful response of the British authorities must have sounded to Garvey like an echo on a broken record: "If conditions there are so bad, Jamaicans can return home."

More disturbing news was to follow. From Black veterans he learned that Black Jamaican and Barbadian troops in the British West India Regiments[2] had been used

---

2. The British West India Regiment[s] (BWIR) has a long, sordid history. Originally formed in the late 18th century, composed of former slaves led by white officers and non commissioned officers (NCOs), it saw action against the United States in the War of 1812. The unit was expanded after 1836 — three years after the abolition of British colonial slavery— with Afrikans taken from aboard "slavers" seized on the high seas by British patrols, raising the establishment's total troop strength to 1500. The gesture was not altruistic. The pressing need to defend an extensive global empire, long-term overseas duty (in some cases as much as 20 years or more), filthy barrack conditions, low or no pay or pension, flogging for minor offences, massive desertions and the incredibly high death toll of white officers and NCOs due to tropical diseases, led even the lowest orders of British society to shun military service. The solution to these problems, although very unpopular at the time, was to enlist larger numbers of "natives" in the service of the Crown. In 1840 the BWIR, which then consisted of two regiments composed mostly of Blacks from the empire's Caribbean territories and a small number from

to crush the rightful resistance of indigenous Afrikans who fought valiantly to defend their birthright from imperial theft. Infamous among these struggles was the last of the Asante Wars (1887-1900) against British Imperial forces, where the steady crack of machine gunfire tore to shreds — in piles waist high — the brave sons of Kumasi. Further informed by vivid reports from Black seamen who had sailed the far reaches of the globe, a broader, more tragic view of the Black world was unfolding.

In 1912 Garvey departed for England, intent upon broadening his perspectives even further. His time was maximized. He attended lectures at Berbeck College, University of London, made regular visits to the House of Commons, studied at the city's magnificent libraries, and spoke at the Hyde Park famous "Speakers Corner." He also traveled to Scotland, Ireland, France, Italy, Spain, Austria, Hungary and Germany. In England, he secured a job with the *African Times and Orient Review* published in London by an indigenous Afrikan Duse Mohamed Ali, a scholar, brilliant propagandist and world traveler who agitated for Afrikan independence. He became a Garvey mentor, enlightening him of Afrika's antiquity, its glorious history, topography, people, mineral wealth, and tremendous potential. Duse also informed on the brutalities of the continuing Arab slave trade, of how Islam came to dominate the continent's northern and eastern regions. He

---

the US, were relocated to Sierra Leone and amalgamated with the Royal African Colonial Corp, again composed of indigenous Afrikans, also led by white officers and NCOs. The sphere of operations of this combined unit included Afrika as well as the Caribbean. They were used to put down the Jamaican rebellion of 1865, fight the Sierra Leone Hut Tax War of 1898, the successive Asante Wars, and saw service in Europe and the Afrikan battlefields of WWI. For more about WWI in Afrika refer to *The Great War in Africa: 1914-1918* by Bryon Farwell, New York: W.W. Norton & Co., 1986.

learned of Afrika's present configuration as a result of the Berlin Conference (November 13, 1884 to February 26, 1885), at which England, France, Germany, Portugal, Spain and Belgium, with Turkey and the United States of America as onlooking, willing accomplices agreed to bring "order" to their ongoing theft of Afrika – a gentleman's agreement that the European imperial powers would "respect" each other's "legitimate" territorial claims. Duse pulled no punches when it came to Afrika's then condition. Slavery, degradation, rampant European domination and brutal exploitation ruled every corner of the Mother continent. The Afrikan race nowhere found a safe haven. Black life was extirpated; the whole race had been brought to heel.

A much enlightened and reinvigorated Garvey returned to Jamaica in June 1914, one month before the outbreak of World War I, his mind filled with ideas of enterprise and the establishing of what he referred to then as the Universal Improvement and Negro Conservation Association and African Communities League, an organization for the betterment of Afrikans (Blacks) at home and abroad. Five days after arrival Garvey launched the Association in Kingston. The Association was officially founded on 1st August 1914, chosen since that date marked the anniversary of the abolition of Afrikan enslavement in the British West Indies.

It met with lukewarm response. Many better-off Blacks disliked "Negro" in the Association's title. Not knowing much about themselves, they associated the word with everything low and filthy. They preferred to be called the *less* offensive, "Colored."The island's Whites, on the other hand, feared the mass organizing of Blacks, that such unity represented a power shift that would loosen and ultimately destroy the grip of white power privilege.

At first, Garvey's efforts were confined to Kingston. After a year of organizing, his following only amounted to about 100. It wasn't until he lectured at his hometown, St. Ann's Bay, that the appeal took hold.

While in London Garvey had, along with numerous other books, read Booker T. Washington's autobiography, *Up From Slavery*. It impacted Garvey profoundly and fueled his clarion call which birthed the UNIA in Jamaica. Its text had welled in Garvey the imperative questions: "Where is the Black man's government? Where is his King and Kingdom? Where is his President, his country, and his ambassador, his army, navy, his men of big affairs?" And not finding them, true to his resolve he declared, "I shall create them." Amid the swirl of organizing activity he further, recalling its text and mission of Tuskegee Institute, set the establishment of technical colleges across the breadth of Jamaica as a UNIA primary goal. He wrote to Booker T. The elder educator responded warmly and invited Garvey to come to the United States of America. Unfortunately, before Garvey could set sail the able Booker T. in 1915 died at age 53.

News of Booker T. Washington's transition did not deter Garvey. Saddened, he proceeded with his planned journey, undaunted. Besides, he had read much about the Republic and wanted to see the raucous giant for himself. He had planned a five-month speaking tour to black areas to raise money for his new UNIA,[3] then return home. He arrived in New York in 1916. After a bout with pneumonia Garvey was on his feet and soon undertaking a breathtaking US speaking tour. He made time to meet and befriend

3. At this point the histories are not clear. It appears that sometime before Garvey set sail for the US, the word "Conservation" was omitted from the title. And thus it became the Universal Negro Improvement Association and African Communities League.

some of the country's leading Black intellectuals and race leaders, many of whom he found wanting, self-serving and lacking in character. His tour through 38 states left him all the wiser, but disappointed. While some Blacks had achieved a narrow measure of progress, their masses were still mired in poverty, lacked education,[4] beset with racism and a host of psychological and physical diseases, and were staggering under massive unemployment – not far from the lash of whips.

Garvey's arrival in Harlem, New York, was an auspicious one. New York was then a port city, a growing center of finance, trade and communication to rival London. As New York's newly created Black quarter, Harlem was swelling with Black refugees from Southern oppression and migrating Blacks from the Caribbean. Harlem's intellectual life bloomed. Artists, writers and musicians gathered there to express their talents in a way not possible in any other climate. There were a number of "race groups," everything from neo-Egyptian mystics to revolutionaries advocating violent overthrow, whose appeals could be heard on any day of the week broadcast from atop speakers' ladders or soap boxes. Garvey sunk himself into this contrasting vibrant environment of wealth and poverty, culture and bawdiness – and awakening. It wasn't long before he was lecturing and joining the soapbox orators. The years of erudition and elocution had paid off. The people of Harlem embraced his message of race pride and race liberation. His paean alit the masses: "Up you mighty race! You can accomplish what you will!"

The year 1917 saw the establishment of the Harlem branch of the UNIA, which boasted a growth of two

4. In 1910 only 45 percent of US Blacks had attended school and out of this number, few got beyond the fifth grade. Those that did were often poorly trained.

thousand members in two months. The organization had found fertile soil. The year 1918 saw the incorporation of the African Communities League, the business arm of the UNIA. That year also saw the birth of the *Negro World,* a well-written, well-edited Pan-Afrikan news and nationalist propaganda vehicle which became the most widely read Black weekly in the world. The pugnacious paper was published in three languages, namely English, Spanish and French. In its early days the *Negro World* was given away for free, slipped under the doors of Harlem residences at sunrise. By 1919, the UNIA had branches in thirty states, while others sprang up in Central and South America, the Spanish- and English-speaking Caribbean and blossomed on the Mother continent, Afrika, where it skipped down the coast to influence the young founders of the Afrikan National Congress in far off South Afrika.[5] Before the dawn of 1920 the organization's ranks had swollen to over a million members, and would in subsequent years rise to well over 6 million, numbers which have not been equaled since by any Black mass organization. America had become a grander platform for his global plans.

The year 1920 would prove to be unparalleled in the history of Pan-Afrikanism. For that entire August Garvey staged in New York City the first of six International Conventions of the Negro People of the World. At the opening session held at Madison Square Garden, 25,000 delegates packed the arena with crowds spilling into the streets outside. Present were delegates from every corner of the globe. The impact of the convention's many resolutions and declarations are still with us. Termed the Black Bill of Rights, the numerous resolutions included: that Black history be taught in schools; that lynching and racial

5. The South Afrikan branches were the most thoroughly organized of all Afrikan divisions.

discrimination be brought to an end; that Afrika belonged to the Afrikans; and that Tricolors of Afrika, the Red, the Black, the Green be adopted as the standard of the race. The assembly also elected Garvey as the President General of the UNIA, and the Provisional President of Afrika. The last day of the Convention was declared a national holiday for Blacks. Such was the magnitude of the UNIA that a parallel convention lasting the same 31 days occurred in Port of Spain, Trinidad, attended by delegates unable to attend the one in New York.

Wherever the organization took root, so too did its voice, the *Negro World*, which became a thorn in the side of the imperialist powers who pulled all stops to stymy or eradicate the paper's appeal. Indeed, in much of Afrika, all of Europe and Great Britain, the Southern states of the US, the Caribbean, Central and South America, to have been caught reading a copy of the "subversive weekly" was a punishable offense, often resulting in hard jail time or worse. Nothing the imperialist governments tried, including seizing bundles of cleverly concealed papers smuggled aboard even their own ships bound for lands adjacent and afar, was completely successful. The liberating message borne on the pages of the *Negro World* infiltrated even the most tightly surveilled borders, reaching as far as Nyasaland (modern Malawi) where it penetrated a defensive ring established by the British Foreign Office.

The organizing and consciousness-raising of the world's exploited and despised Black population did not proceed without determined, aggressive opposition. Hostility on the part of capitalist interests within Europe (Britain especially) and the United States were to be expected: after all, it was their ill-gotten gains that a triumphant UNIA would attempt to reclaim. US authorities conspired to bar Garvey reentry from the Caribbean when on company business acquiring funds for the Black Star Line steamship company. Garvey was cognizant that not all Blacks would buy into his program of "do for self" and self-determination. But to be viciously opposed by the NAACP, Black labor leaders, leading churchmen, intellectuals and almost every black newspaper of note, came as a rude awakening, a searing realization that the struggle for true liberation would set, to the death, Black against Black — fang and claw. In this matter there are no bloodless roads.

The political environment in which the UNIA functioned within the United States black enclaves were in a word, toxic, poisoned by three centuries of pervasive racial oppression and conditioned subservience. Yet, in spite of this outpouring of resentment against the ridiculed visionary, the "charlatan" in their midst, Garvey's appeal reached the hearts and minds of millions of downtrodden Blacks (at home and abroad, as evidenced by the maps and charts thus presented), who were otherwise untouched by the protest methods of the then established leadership, for whom a resurgent Afrika simply was not in their vision. This so sadly remains to this very day as we witness the present strain of accommodating "race leaders" champion social and economic policies designed to keep Afrika a land of beggars, forever at the beck and call of Western interests.

Afrikans at home and aboard saw in Garvey's appeal a universal truth: If the race was to advance, it could not do so clinging to the coattails of its oppressors or solely on the achievement of a handful of great men and women, no matter how elevated their status or how deep their pockets. Advancement depends, they reasoned, on lifting the majority of the people into the sphere of prosperity; thus life would have meaning and purpose beyond material goods. Garvey sought to achieve this by embarking upon numerous economic ventures that would not only give the race a sense of pride, but also the discipline necessary to compete within the treacherous currents of a rapidly changing world. He encouraged entrepreneurship.

The Garvey Movement, through investing by its worldwide membership, acquired hotels, restaurants, factories, universities of higher learning, printing plants, publishing companies,[6] newspapers, transoceanic steamship lines, to name a few. In addition, it established civil services (employment offices, job training, courts, passport services), health care services (under the Black Cross nurses), regiments (the African Legions), all as foundational springboards necessary to the construction of the new continental Afrikan nation and homeland. The UNIA in fact entered into negotiations and even sent supplies to the emerging Republic of Liberia, West Afrika, as the beachhead for the establishing of the Pan-Afrikan vision on the continent, only to be thwarted by a coalition of Firestone Rubber Company and US governmental pressure on the Liberian government.

6. Myopia is a deficiency of the eye, the inability to see clearly at a distance, or in this case, the lack of foresight. During the Harlem Renaissance many of the leading Black writers protested vigorously and complained without end that white publishing concerns would not, solely based on racial discrimination (today's *profiling*) publish or even review their works. This of course was true and in many cases remains so. But what these august champions of race pride seemed to have overlooked, or could not see through their obsequious begging, was the UNIA's publishing house, run by the African Communities League, located squarely in the heart of 135th Street, Harlem. At the time, books, pamphlets, newspapers and other materials were typeset, printed, bound and shipped to distant places on the globe through the UNIA's book department. With over six million card-carrying members of the UNIA, the literary lights surely would have found a ready market for their products, without having to depend on white largesse.

If it is as the ancients have said that "the nature of a man can be judged by the enemies he makes," then Garvey stands head-and-shoulders above all others. For his entire political life he stood resolute against Euro-imperialist powers. He repulsed attempts by the Communist Party to coopt the UNIA, which by the mid 1920s had greater global reach than Lenin's struggling workers Paradise. Concurrently Garvey went toe to toe, traded thrust and perry with saboteurs, opportunists, and reactionary leaders like the NAACP, the one group who if properly aligned with UNIA objectives would have benefitted greatly from a liberated Afrika and the defeat of white rule.

The race leaders of the time labeled Garvey a "dreamer" that had duped the masses, fleeced their pockets and was leading them toward highly unattainable goals. We now know differently.

The year the Harlem division of the UNIA was founded, 1917, the imperialist powers were near the close of a tragic and costly "war to end all wars" (WWI) in which the flower of their youths was squandered in bloody, mud-filled trenches that meandered across the entire width of Europe, from the Swiss Alps to the frigid waters of the Baltic Sea. The death toll was tremendous: France lost 1.7million; the British Empire, 908,371; the United States of America, 126,000; and Germany, 2 million. The total number of *dead* and *wounded* for all combatants —from Austria-Hungary, Belgium, Bulgaria, Greece, Italy, Japan, Montenegro, Portugal, Rumania, Russia, Serbia, Turkey, Caribbean and continental Afrikan conscripts and volunteers from all colonies — was *8 million* and *21 million* respectively. These figures do not reflect the untold millions of noncombatants who perished as a result of war-triggered famine and disease, and the millions of widows who were also bellum's victims. Then, as if the god of war and retribution was yet appeased, the influenza pandemic of 1918 struck, killing 20 million worldwide, 550,000 in the US alone. The cost of the conflict, in monetary terms, was well above $200 billion in 1918 dollars. Europe was a shadow of its former self, economically- and people-depleted, and gone, too, was the smug illusion that Western civilization had lifted itself above the station of savage.

France had lost her much-valued industrial sector in the opening stages of the war and those of her youth who were not shell-shocked were war-weary; their anxiety-filled eyes gazed out across acre upon acre of newly planted crosses. Once a leading industrial power, a shining center of philosophy and science, Germany was shattered. Her sons, who had had the martial spirit drummed into them since childhood, limped home, ragged, to find famine, disease, economic ruin, social unrest and the mean ghost of despotism lurking within the shadows of despair. And although England was considered among the victors, her army had been broken, bled white — a ghastly wound clearly visible to the yearning eyes of the oppressed nations within her empire. The house of cards was set to fall.

The United States, a late comer to the war (1917-1918), entered the war years (1914-1918) a debtor nation, its industry in the hands of foreign shareholders. She possessed a small army of 107,641 men with outdated weapons, a weak decentralized government, was plagued with worker dissatisfaction, ethnic strife which bordered on national chaos, and an insidious drug and alcohol problem that ate away at the nation's human potential. Bubbling beneath these conditions was yet another current that would swell into a flood; Blacks fleeing Southern terror —

the hangman's noose (the KKK), torture, rape, peonage, eternal debt and scratching out a hard existence on mean scrabbles of land. Flooding of the Mississippi and the boll-weevil's devastation of king cotton exacerbated horrendous conditions. Whole families headed north to the dark precincts of Philadelphia, Detroit, Chicago, St. Louis, Pittsburgh, Cleveland, Cincinnati, Newark, and Harlem in New York to fill jobs created by the shortage of European immigrant labor. The war had stemmed that flow since Europe needed all hands to fight or to work.

As the war progressed and the need for everything from cotton to high-grade steel intensified, the supply lines sunk into every continent and sucked vital minerals into the cauldron, altering the nature of American society forever. By 1916 a small segment of the US economy had grown astonishingly wealthy from war profits so much so that the country's industry passed over completely into American hands. The army had increased to 223,500 in 1915, then to just under three million by the end of hostilities in 1918. Driven by fear of military invasion, foreign ideologies (Communism and Anarchy), chaos created by ethnic diversity (more than 100 languages and dialects were spoken across the country) and the potentially destabilizing power of the giant "money monopolies" which at the time owned 40% of US industries, government expanded to deal with these problems. It grew until intruding into the lives of individuals and organizations in a way that it never had or could before. In spite of government-sponsored programs aimed at Americanization (a massive national effort to impose white Anglo-Saxon ethics upon the immigrant populations) to create a great "melting pot," bitter ethnic rivalries, race hatred and labor strikes, some amounting to small wars, continued.

Afrika, which had contributed greatly to the war in both men and material[7] — over 80,000 of her sons lay dead on French soil[8] — was thrown into a state of upheaval. During the conflict Afrikan troops killed each other in the name of their colonial masters in small intense battles that ranged across the width and depth of Afrika. When the imperialists went to war, their colonies took up arms also. At war's end, Afrikans in every territory found themselves trapped in an inflation-ridden economy and consequently in worse economic condition than when the war began in 1914. Many had hoped that dogged loyalty to the "mother country," their colonial overlords, would bring rewards,

7. It put to rest forever the romantic Hollywood image of long winding lines of Afrikan head porters walking gracefully off into the sunset — chanting. In reality, Afrikans hated the work, even in peacetime, and in most cases would not do the boring, neck-straining labor even for money. During the First World War over one million men, women and children were pressed into service through conscription, and as could be expected, protests and bloody rebellions resulted. Whole villages fled into the bush to avoid porterage, and to save their sons from being drawn into the war they called "thangata" — work without real benefit. In 1917, German missionary Dr. Albert Schweitzer reported seeing the "emaciated bodies" of bearers lying beside the roads. The total death toll resulting from the forced labor campaigns will never be known, but as an example here, we can examine the figures from Nyasaland (modern day Malawi) in East Afrika, where from 1914-1918 the longest struggles of the war took place. The total number of laborers supplied (ages 16-40) was just over 200,000; the deaths resulting from disease, food shortages and medical neglect amounted to 100,000. This does not include those left behind in the villages to fend for themselves — the elderly, the infirm and very young children whose lives were also cut short by disease and the onset of drought in 1917.

8. Note that Americans of black hue, the 369th Regiment, also died, clad in French uniforms in World War I, forbidden service in the US military due to the standing race policy of apartheid/segregation in the United States in general and the military in particular. They, like their continental Afrikan brothers, died preserving "freedoms" and making the world "safe for democracy" while they were being deprived these rights at home.

win them a place at the "table of humankind." But for all their suffering and dying, Afrikans got absolutely nothing – materially. Because of the war's insatiable manpower needs, many village-bound Afrikans traveled abroad for the first time and were shocked into a new reality. Seeing strange lands, they shrewdly took inventory of what others had and they had not. They saw in fact how the sum total of their slave-like labor at home had enriched others and left continental Afrikans in a constant state of want, without control over their lives or their future. Their exchanging of ideas with people previously never even dreamt of was an education in itself. They saw, too, how "Christian Civilization" made war, saw it use every fiendish device conceived by modern industrial science to rip the souls of its baptized sons: blindness and choking resulting from poison gas attacks; immolation by flame thrower; the heaving of the earth under mountain-shattering barrages which often lasted for hours; the conveyor belt-like mass death produced by batteries of clattering machine guns; the first brutal forms of tanks, as they lumbered out across no man's land to break the stalemate; and, high above the field of carnage, in the sacred domain once ruled by the gods and the birds, the crucifix-like silhouettes of aircraft rained bombs and fire upon the living and the dead caged in the putrid mud below. The Great War had taught them yet another poignant, indelible lesson – that they could kill White men in large numbers!

Bitter that the service and loyalty they had shown their European colonial masters had yielded no recompense, Afrikan veterans, students and workers reconsidered their place in the existing order. As a result, protests, strikes, and open rebellions against colonial rule accelerated and reverberated with the Garvey-inspired paean, "Africa for the Africans!"

Given this state of affairs, the conclusion of the First World War was an opportune time for Blacks the world-over to press for Afrikan independence. Admittedly, even with the war's ravages, the US and Europe still had considerable technological advantages over Afrika that would have made armed conflict suicidal, as in many cases it was. But, that was not what Garvey suggested. A pragmatist and tactician, he stressed preparation — ORGANIZATION. "One God! One Aim! One Destiny!" he repeated as the greatest weapon available to the race and the surest means to change the standing order of things. He detested riots and warned against such "foolish self-destructive acts." If coordinated disciplined mass efforts in the form of worker sit-down strikes, boycotts, persistent agitation, large-scale voter turnout and economic self-reliance were applied directly to the cause of Afrikan freedom, then the imperial powers surely would have had to yield, not only from the demands of Blacks, but from the added weight of other oppressed peoples around the world who were also demanding their freedom and applying pressure to the rotten imperial edifice.

The post-war world was a time of revolution. The imperial powers may not have immediately quit Afrika, but given their vulnerable post-war condition and the need to maintain the fragile web of international commerce and trade which bound all nations together, concessions would have been made and thereby at least two generations of Afrikans spared further harsh colonial rule thus hastening the process of liberation. And, Ethiopia would have been spared.[9]

9. It's common knowledge that the forerunner of the United Nations, the League of Nations, failed. But for the purpose of this introduction, attention needs to be paid to the opening session of the Paris Peace Conference held on January 18, 1918, at which the "spoils of

At the time, given its global reach (see map 1, World Distribution of UNIA Branches) the UNIA was the *only* Pan-Afrikan organization strategically positioned to carry out such an effort. All that was needed was the considerable scientific, technical, intellectual, economic and political talents possessed by the Afrikan-American elite to bring added expertise and discipline to strengthen the organizational infrastructure of the UNIA. Instead, goaded by fear and envy, the myopic race leaders – spearheaded by the NAACP – chose to mount a "Garvey Must Go" campaign that allied with relentless pressure on the part of the US government and J. Edgar Hoover's surveillance of Garvey and top UNIA officers: "The fault, dear Brutus, lies not in the stars. But in ourselves, that we are underlings."

war" or what should be done with the colonies of the defeated powers, and colonies in general, was put before the delegates. At the conference, US President Woodrow Wilson in his plan for the League of Nations, "the New World Order," proposed a three-stage mandate system: Class A, Arab lands, Class C, islands of the Pacific and Class B, which concerns us here, covered most of Afrika and called for placing these territories under League supervision (policing) so that the "natives" received fair treatment, i.e., put an end to the colonial misconduct and speed up the process of self-rule. This part of Wilson's plan was rapidly agreed upon by the delegates representing the victorious nations. The popular misconception that Liberia and Ethiopia were Afrika's only independent states, is of course a myth in the broad strategic sense. Liberia was under the strong arm of US rubber interests [Firestone], and although Menelik II proved successful at defeating Italian expansion into his country at the Battle of Adowa (modern Adwa) in 1896, large portions of the old Ethiopian Empire remained in hostile foreign hands: Italian Somaliland, British Somaliland. French Somaliland, Eritrea and continued Egyptian occupation of the northern region denied the country its extensive coastline. Landlocked, Ras Tafari, crowned Emperor under the name Haile Selassie I, on November 2nd, 1928, embarked on a modernization program but was complicated by the onset of the Great Depression of 1929, and other international factors which invited further Italian aggression from 1935-1941. Ironically, Ethiopia's security lay in the hands of an alerted and united UNIA-led Afrikan Diaspora (as advocated on the pages of Garvey's *Negro World*) able to bring concerted political pressure to bear on the League of Nations and the seat of growing world power, the United States of America.

As a result of these actions Garvey was speciously charged with using the mail to defraud by selling "worthless stock" in the Black Star Line, the UNIA's steamship company. The government produced only one intimidated witness with a tremendously flawed memory and an empty envelope as proof of the $5.00 stock purchase. Furthermore, there was no letter on Black Star Line or UNIA stationery, no stock certificate or proof of payment. On 21st June 1923 after 11½ hours of deliberation, which included the judge's unsolicited redirect to the jury on the costs in time and money of a possible verdict of mistrial or hung jury, Garvey *alone* was convicted, his three co-defendants acquitted on the same evidence, same testimony. Normally the sentence for mail fraud was one year, but Judge Julian Mack, an NAACP member, threw the book at Garvey with a maximum sentence of 5 years, a $1,000 fine, and ordered to pay court costs of approximately $5,000. They had bagged their tiger.

He was immediately removed to the Tombs Prison in New York City. Released after three months, pending appeal, Garvey continued his business operations, though barred from venturing outside prescribed geographic boundaries. He lost on appeal. Sentenced in 1925, the railroaded Garvey had his sentence commuted after two years, not because of altruism or good behavior, but because of mounting pressure from angry UNIA members. At one Harlem demonstration alone, 150,000 people were counted filling the streets.

In January of 1927 Garvey was released from Atlanta Prison, then summarily deported to native Jamaica from New Orleans, Louisiana. At New Orleans he gave a farewell address before a gathering of 5,000 tearful supporters. History has it that on that day the heavens opened; it rained profusely as the ship *Saramacca* slipped out to sea to the song "God bless our President" bellowing from the hearts of his loyal followers. Banished, he would never again set foot in the United States of America, despite many petitions for reentry. He was relegated to administering UNIA affairs from overseas, a near-impossible task for anyone save Marcus Garvey. He had departed America a warrior wounded, but not vanquished.

True to his solemn oath, ". . . I have sworn by you and my God to serve to the end of all time, the wreck of matter and the crash of worlds," Marcus Garvey never surrendered. Imbued with a profound love for his people, he continued his blistering work for Black liberation, first in Jamaica where he entered electoral politics dominated by the colonial British. To effect a favorable political climate he founded the *Blackman* (1929-31) and *New Jamaican* (1932-33) newspapers, and a magazine, the *Black Man,* as vehicles to rally his local following. He further traveled the Caribbean, Central America, and in Canada across the border from Buffalo, he established links with UNIA divisions in New York. As a lasting tribute to his members he inaugurated the *School of Afrikan Philosophy* at Toronto, Canada, in September of 1937. He taught the first *Course of Afrikan Philosophy* himself, a grueling leadership program, not for the faint of heart or the unambitious. Garvey continued relentlessly, passing his final years in London advocating in Hyde Park for his people. It must have been rewarding to him to see the issues on whose righteousness he stood, was persecuted and prosecuted for, become those quintessential initiatives co-opted and championed by his detractors and successors. How he must have felt a sense of vindication for standing on the right side of History!

A life lived cannot be without error or regret. No plaster saint, was Marcus Garvey; he made miscalculations. In spite of this he left us a valuable legacy upon which we, his children, can build. Because of him and the noble doers and thinkers who are his predecessors, we no longer view ourselves through the mangled lens of white supremacy. Afrika is now, in spite of her present troubles, a source of inspiration and the place of our future glory.

The Honorable Marcus Mosiah Garvey joined our noble Ancestors in June of 1940. He was buried in England. As fate would have it, though once castigated and feared in his homeland, his remains were disinterred and re-interred in his native Jamaica in August 1964 at the National Heroes Park. He was by all accounts a man for any century. □

–Joseph Gillians

This synopsis is set to lay the backdrop to the thoughts expressed in the upcoming presentations, *The Legacy of Marcus Garvey* and *Afrikan-centered Consciousness, Personality and Culture as Instruments of Power.* It is also intended to implore the interested to study issues of Black Power and Afrikan-centered consciousness before the 1960s and contrast such with the mind-set and political directions outlined by present leadership. In this look at Garveyism, Dr. Amos Wilson calls to critical view the measuring rod by which all Afrikans must evaluate his or her contribution to the uplift and liberation of Afrikan people everywhere.

We at Afrikan World InfoSystems however regret that because of the constraints of space and time we were not, as of this printing, able to place before the reader a fuller, more detailed account of the life and times of the Honorable Marcus Garvey. There were many more issues we longed to survey. One such musing was that much of what we as a people presently discuss, think of as new, was long ago analyzed and debated on the pages of Garvey's *Negro*

World — even Malcolm X's fiery oratory gleams from its age-yellowed sheets almost verbatim. The intellectual insights of our distinguished elders were both protean and incredibly incisive.

> The numbers of Blacks in jails, prisons and reformatories of the United States, the British West Indian and other colonies and countries, the protectorates and the dominions of Great Britain and France in Africa, is shamefully in excess, proportionately, of all other race groups to the populations. —MARCUS GARVEY, 1919

> [It's] vastly cheaper to build schoolhouses than jails.
> —T. THOMAS FORTUNE, 1900

In other words, the discourse had begun; the wheel has already been invented. Again, we implore the reader to study.

These lectures, transcribed, edited, subtitled and otherwise annotated were delivered in the years 1985 and 1994 respectively, in Brooklyn, New York at the Marcus Garvey Senior Citizen Center and at the assembly hall of the United African Movement. We trust you will find them eye-opening and fitting complements to the much-acclaimed masterpiece *Blueprint for Black Power: A Moral, Political and Economic Imperative for the Twenty-First Century.*

"Up You Mighty Race!
You Can Accomplish What You Will!"

Sababu N. Plata
EXECUTIVE EDITOR

Selected Bibliography

Chandler, D., and I. Becker, 1994. *The Oxford Illustrated History of the British Army*. New York: Oxford University Press.

Crowder, M. 1968. *West Africa Under Colonial Rule*. Evanston: Northwestern University Press.

Edgeman, R.B. 1995. *The Fall of the Asante Empire: The Hundred-Year War for Africa's Gold Coast*. New York: The Free Press.

Ellis, J. 1975 *The Social History of the Machine Gun*. New York. Pantheon Books.

Garvey, A.J. 1968. *Garvey and Garveyism*. Kingston, Jamaica, West Indies: A Jacques Garvey Publisher.

Garvey, A. J., and H.R. Lynch, 1968. *Philosophy and Opinions of Marcus Garvey*, Vols. I and II. New York: Atheneum.

Harries, M., and S. Harries, 1997. *The Last Days of Innocence: America at War, 1917-1918*. New York: Random House.

Martin, T. 1976. *Race First: The Ideological and Organizational Struggles of Marcus Garvey and the Universal Negro Improvement Association*. Dover, Massachusetts: The Majority Press.

_____, 1983. *The Pan-African Connection: From Slavery to Garvey and Beyond*. Dover, Massachusetts: The Majority Press.

_____, *African Fundamentalism: A Literary and Cultural Anthology of Garvey's Harlem Renaissance*. Dover, Massachusetts: The Majority Press.

Martin, T., and C.L. James, 1986. *Message to the People: The Course of African Philosophy*. Dover, Massachusetts: The Majority Press.

O'Connell, R.L. *Of Men and Arms: A History of War Weapons and Aggression*. New York: Oxford University Press.

Perrett, G. 1982. *America in the Twenties: A History*. New York: Simon and Schuster.

Rotberg, R.I., and Ali A. Mazuri, 1970. *Power and Protest in Black Africa*. New York: Oxford University Press.

Strachan, H. 1998. *World War I: A History*. New York: Oxford University Press.

ON MICROFILM, *Negro World 1923-1924 Editions*. New York: Schomburg Collection.

Part One

The Legacy of Marcus Garvey

Part One

I am certainly honored to be asked to speak with you, share a bit with you this afternoon, and certainly to give honor to the Honorable Marcus Garvey. I hope I can do him honor with what I have to say today.

I'd like to make a few preliminary statements. We have the handouts here about the series of lectures I will be doing starting on 17th April and each Friday thereafter for five consecutive Fridays. In that series of lectures, I will be talking about the psychology of self-hatred and self-defeat. I want to go into detail in terms of this kind of psychology because it is so crucial to our current situation and how we arrived at our current situation. The psychology of self-hatred is an issue we must deal with if we are to move forward as a people, since that psychology is so intimately related to everything we do. I'm taking the opportunity in this series of lectures to give an uninterrupted coherent presentation of this psychology which I think is very important for us to know. Our first two lectures will deal with the introjection of self-hatred into the oppressed Afrikan personality, just how does this psychology of self-hatred work? How was it introduced into the Afrikan mind? How does it operate in the Afrikan psyche? What were the particular techniques used by our oppressors to bring about this psychology? We will talk about it in technical detail. The lectures will be somewhat didactic, in the sense that we really want to discuss thoroughly the psychology of the inducement of self-hatred so that we can get into some form of self-understanding. Once we learn the techniques by which self-hatred is implanted, we can arrive at methods for overcoming that psychology as such.

I'd like to take this opportunity to respectfully plug my institution over there at 215 West 125th Street, the Harlem Graphic Arts Center. You are welcomed to come by to see us. I've indicated on a number of occasions that we are trying to put into concrete action the ideology and philosophy of such great leaders as Marcus Garvey and to show that black nationalism is not just an ideology, not just rhetoric, but that it is an ideology that leads to self-actualization and concrete development. We want to show that what we are about philosophically and ideologically actualizes itself in concrete construction and development. We are there planning to overthrow a number of myths; the myth that we as a people cannot work together and build an enterprise that is efficient; the mythology of the so-called black businessperson. We are trying to destroy the myth that one has to deny his or her culture in order to make money or to create wealth. You often hear many of our people saying that they're not about black power but about green power, as if those things can really be separated. The route to green power, or whatever monetary color you want to talk about, is through black power. Consequently, you will see our efforts to try to meld wealth-creation and job-creation with cultural advancement and development. We are not hiding our culture; we are projecting it.

We recognize that European culture has been projected not through lectures but through commercial activities, through trade and through economic development.

European cultural imperialism is the handmaiden of European economic and militaristic imperialism. Ultimately, if we are to advance the culture, we must advance the culture at all levels of our activities, which include our commercial activities as well. It is very important that we succeed since we want to illustrate that when an Afrikan votes and moves in favor of an Afrikan ideology, he's not voting for poverty, he's voting for enrichment, he's not voting for dependency, he's not voting for empty rhetoric and rage: He is voting to do something concrete about his situation. Our success as a business is one of the greatest political statements we can make. We urge you to help us make that statement, along with other sisters and brothers who are in Brooklyn, Bronx and Manhattan who are trying to do the same thing. We talk with each other, work and collaborate with each other in an effort to try to advance the ideology of Afrikan nationalism. So we all need your support.

Garvey and the Structuring of Reality

I want to look for a moment at what I would call the legacy of Marcus Garvey. I want to note personally that it was the reading of *The Philosophy and Opinions of Marcus Garvey* that did so much to transform my own attitudes about myself and my people. Not that I needed to be transformed from an assimilationist/integrationist self-hating position, but that I needed to develop a coherent ideological position. I was fortunate in my own upbringing to have been reared in a black community, to have been educated in black institutions where loving black people and being concerned about the advancement of Afrikan people was just natural. It was something that did not have to be lectured or taught into me; it was just a natural part of my growth and development. However, I must say that with my coming to

New York City, reading the books about Garvey and others, exposing myself to the bookstores, Michaux's bookstore, standing on the corner there with Irvin "Porkchop" Davis (who passed here recently) and hearing other speakers, that sort of put it all in place for me, crystallized my ultimate sense of direction. On my shelf right now is a four-act play about Marcus Garvey. I have one more act to go. Written about 10 or 15 years ago, it's been sitting there. I've been telling myself that I'm going to ultimately get around to finishing that play. So you can see that my spiritual relationship with him has been quite intimate, intimate enough for me in my first writing efforts to seek to dramatize his life and philosophy in such a way that it could advance my own development and advance the growth and development of my people. He has been the center of my life ever since. I certainly see myself as a descendant of Marcus Garvey and what Marcus Garvey was about.

We don't have time today to review the history of Marcus Garvey. Rather than try to recap this history, which I'm sure most of you are familiar with anyway, I'll just take a brief look at some things I think Marcus Garvey left us as an individual, as an organizational person and as a leader of Afrikan people.

Perception One of the major things in the Marcus Garvey legacy was that of his perception of reality. I often talk about reality in my classes and general lectures so that attendees would recognize that at the center of one's adjustment to the world, at the center of one's ability to deal with the world, to change the world to suit one's advantage, is a knowledge of reality. The very essence of pathology, whether political, ideological, economic, social, or psychological, is a lack of knowledge of reality. How can one deal with reality if one does not know what it is? How can you deal with reality if you're blind to it or if it is distorted?

It is somewhat interesting that the brain is locked up in the darkness of the skull, yet the brain is the central unit that guides our behavior. It guides that behavior based on the information it receives from our senses. Therefore, our senses must relay to the brain an accurate knowledge of reality. This is the only knowledge, ultimately, that the brain gets from the outside world. The brain, using its innate capacities, such as reasoning capacities, comparative capacities, basic knowledge, memory and experience, uses the information given to it by the senses to determine how the person is going to deal and cope with reality, how the individual is going to shape reality to its own purposes. Therefore, if that information is distorted, then the brain determines behavior on that distorted information and the individual is maladjusted. This is the case then with a people.

It is necessary for a people, if they are coping with reality, if they are trying to advance themselves, to know that reality. They need sensors and people who can tell what that reality is, who can inform them as to the nature of that reality such that the decisions the group must make in determining how it will behave, how it will shape its destiny, can be based on the real, not on the unreal. In Marcus Garvey, I see this great sensor, this great seer who informed us of the real world in which we existed. Not of a dream world, not of a world of wishful thinking, not a world distorted by hope, but a world that was seen as it is, a world that was sometimes brutally projected to us as a people so that we could use that knowledge to advance our interests as such. This is a legacy from Garvey that we must continue. Regardless of our pain, regardless of our discouragement, regardless as to what may be going on, we must be determined to look reality in the face and to use that reality as a base and foundation of our behavior.

Perception and Self-Knowledge I also see in the legacy of Marcus Garvey the legacy of self-knowledge. Teachers, wise men and women from eons past have indicated that the foundations of sanity and wisdom rest on a knowledge of self: knowing self. We know that at the very center of Egyptian philosophy was the admonition, *Know Thyself.* That is the essence of wisdom. Garvey thus recognized that a lack of knowledge, an amnesia about who and what we are, is pathological. We recognize today in psychology that amnesia is a pathological state of mind; that a people who suffer from a lack of knowledge of themselves and of their history, *a lack of knowledge of their creation,* are a people who suffer from a loss of identity. We recognize, as Garvey recognized, that this lack of self-knowledge was deliberately induced into the mind and psyche of black people. We could not be Afrikans and slaves at the same time; we could not hold onto our Afrikan identity, our Afrikan selves, knowledge of our Afrikan culture, and be enslaved — the subordinates of another people. It is only when that knowledge is removed, erased, degraded, stolen, taken and distorted that we lose our identity. It is then that an identity is placed upon us by another people and by external forces. Therefore, a lack of self-knowledge is a lack of self-awareness. A lack of self-awareness is an insensitivity to the self. But an insensitivity in the self is also an insensitivity to reality and to the outside world. Without the sensitivity of the outside world and the self, we are left to blindly stumble from one point to another.

Ultimately, self-knowledge in its deepest sense is a knowledge of others. We cannot really get to know ourselves deeply without in essence knowing our enemies and friends and without ultimately knowing the Creator, in whatever form or fashion. It reasons that to know the self ultimately involves moving beyond the self and seeing the world from the vantage point of universalism. Consequently we see in Marcus Garvey, in his efforts to rescue us from the pathology of racism, the putting of major emphasis on self-knowledge and self-knowing. We must recognize today that if we are to regain our Afrikan selves, we must then deeply engage in self-knowledge and self-knowing.

Perception and Lack of Self-Knowledge In psychology, we also recognize that at the center of pathology is the individual's inability to control the self. One of the amazing things about the human mind when one looks at it from the point of view of the so-called unconscious, is that the individual who does not know himself and does not know reality, is the individual who escapes from self-knowledge, is an individual who does not know the roots and bases of his actions. He is an individual who seems to be determined by external forces (or by internal forces) of which he has little or no knowledge. He is often constantly puzzled by his own behavior. He is often a wonderment to himself. He struggles against impulses, desires and wishes over which he has little or no control because he has, in his escape from self-knowing and reality, conceded his self-control and given it over to someone else. In releasing his identity and permitting another to place an identity within his psyche, he has at the same time placed in the hands of that other the ability to control his behavior.

We see in Marcus Garvey's legacy that if we are to control our destiny, we then must control ourselves. We must enter into a phase where the control of our behavior comes under the domination of our will. The essence in many psychotherapeutic approaches is to make the individual aware of the unconscious forces, wishes and impulses that are determining his behavior against his will. And in making these forces conscious, the individual can bring them under conscious control; the individual can bring his behavior under the dominant control of reason and logic. He, then, is not a victim of his emotions. He is not swept by emotions and feelings only, but his emotions serve his interest. His emotions are *his* handmaidens and he is not just one who is swept along helter-skelter by feelings and impulses.

We see in Marcus Garvey the ultimate psychotherapist, one who is revealing and who reveals the unconscious controls, the controls that were implanted outside of our consciousness by our enemies and oppressors. Yet, despite those controls being outside of our consciousness, they were manipulating our behavior to our own disadvantage. In bringing those unconscious forces into consciousness, he made it possible for us to bring those forces under our control, rule, logic, rationality, and under the control of the ideology of nationalism. This is the legacy that still lives today.

Often we see in the neurotic and pathological individual, one who has little self-esteem and self-acceptance. The acceptance of reality, which I referred to in the beginning, ultimately must be the acceptance of one's self. The acceptance of reality, as Marcus Garvey recognized and projected, ultimately must mean the acceptance of our Afrikanicity, the acceptance of the fact that we are an Afrikan people. It seems a bit simple when we state it. It seems a bit obvious. However, when we engage in psychotherapy, we recognize that sometimes we have the patient who comes into the office who is intellectually aware and can quite often lecture the therapist in terms of theoretical ideas and the theoretical grounds for his therapeutic work, but who has not recognized and confronted himself emotionally, who has not really in his heart accepted what he knows. What I am stating here is that while we may recognize superficially and intellectually that it is important we accept the reality of our Afrikan history, we must recognize deeply in our hearts, in the very bottoms of our psyches, our Afrikanicity.

Much of the pathology of Afrikan people today is this vain hope that somehow we will be able to escape our Afrikan heritage, that somehow the white man will become color blind and will not see us for whom and what we are, that somehow we will be looked upon as some kind of abstraction – as just a man. Not as an Afrikan man, not as a black man, but as a man, a human being *only* – without culture, without recognition, without identity. Too many of us want to shed our Afrikanicity for this kind of bogus, abstract existence, which is no existence at all, and which is the ultimate acceptance of invisibility. We must recognize that we are an Afrikan people and we will be Afrikan people to the end of time – and we must accept all that goes with that. We must accept the good, the bad, and all of the possibilities that go with being Afrikan. We must accept the fact that this white man is never going to accept us totally, and get used to the idea. Hope is a wonderful thing in some senses, but it can be pathological in others. The neurotic individual uses hope in a pathological way. He lives in hope and does not know when to give it up. *There's a time that hope has to be given up*; when one looks at reality and recognizes reality for what it is, and one accepts certain aspects of that reality and moves on it. The hope that this white man is going to accept you as one of his own, is one of those hopes that you must give up.

The hope and the dream that you're going to be holding hands with little white boys and girls; that the white man is going to feed your children before he feeds his own; that he's going to clothe you before he clothes his own; that he's going to give up his ill-gotten gains and wealth in the name of some kind of bogus brotherhood or classless society, is a vain hope. Give it up! Turn it loose! When you turn it loose you will see a growth and development of self. It would mean then an acceptance of self. We see this in Marcus Garvey as he got us to accept and tried to get us to accept the reality of ourselves and the reality of our Afrikanicity.

He recognized, as we must recognize today, that we cannot get self-acceptance through another people acceptance us as one of them. Self-acceptance can only be achieved through the self. We must not wait for our enemies to approve of us and to so-call accept us as a way of accepting ourselves. Because, ladies and gentlemen, our enemies, their very lives and very way of life depend upon our non self-acceptance. If the foundation of their very culture and the foundation of their economic, political and social system is one that is founded upon the subordination of black people, then you must recognize that they are not going to give that up. For it would be like giving up their very lives and their very existence itself. Therefore, for us to wait around in the vain hope that through their acceptance we will come to accept ourselves, is to wait for nothing, because we will gain nothing as a result of this kind of illusion.

We see in Marcus Garvey and in his legacy a confrontation with self-acceptance and all that implies. He helped us to accept ourselves through a study of our history and a study of our past. But we will see that he did not get stuck in history, that he was very much in the present and very much into the future. He recognized, as we must recognize today, that we cannot advance the interests of our people through the imitation of our oppressors. Sort of reminds me of that movie *Imitation of Life,* the assuming that your oppressor represents life. One of the things that we must recognize is that our oppressor represents death; our oppressor is deadly. One of the things that impressed me most when I went to graduate school and really had my first real contact with the white educational establishment was that these people are dead. There's death around them somewhere, which is the reason they are deadly as a people, why every advance of knowledge for them is an advancement in the knowledge of destruction. Every advancement in knowledge is an advancement in the ability to kill and destroy the earth, kill and destroy nature, kill and destroy others, rape and rob the earth of its wealth, people and life forms, so much so that now they are having great difficulty even reproducing themselves. At the very center of their lives is death and destruction. We cannot imitate a people who are our oppressors. And we have this kind of silliness that goes on in this system today. You are going to complain on one hand about these racist people, about how they enslaved us, exploited us, discriminated against us, how they lynched and pillaged us, and then turn right around and see their behavior as something to be emulated and imitated.

Ladies and gentlemen, if you imitate and identify with your oppressor, since the oppressor treats us with disdain and degradation, treats us with destructive impulses and desires, will not the imitation of our oppressor now mean that we would then be an imitation of this oppressive being and thus we would engage also in self-destruction and self-degradation? If we behave the way our oppressor behaves then, won't we also engage in self-oppression? If we think the way our oppressor thinks, won't we think about ourselves the way our oppressor thinks about us? If we talk the way our oppressor talks, won't we curse ourselves the way our oppressor curses us?

When we ride these subways day in and day out and look at the behavior of our people in these communities, we can see a people imitating their oppressor. In imitating their oppressor they perform the work of the oppressor in terms of self-destruction and self-abnegation. Imitation of the oppressor is then equivalent to the treatment of the self and one's fellows just as the oppressor would treat us. It is equal to the treatment of the self and the group in a destructive manner. It equals the lack of self-respect and respect for the group, since the oppressor lacks respect for us as individuals and as a group. If our oppressors exploit us, then the imitation of our oppressor means self-exploitation. Consequently we see in the legacy of Marcus Garvey, a moving away from the imitation of our oppressors and a moving toward the identification with all that is Afrikan.

Marcus Garvey recognized as well that we must, as people, love one another. As all great teachers have taught, love is the foundation for any group's cohesiveness and unity of purpose. Love is the greatest inhibitor of aggression and internal conflict. It is the means by which the group cares and shares for itself its resources. It is the means by which the group harnesses its resources and defends itself against the incursions of its enemies. We have a philosophy here today that often only permits love to take place in terms of people outside of ourselves, in terms of people external to ourselves. At the center of the integrationist movement is this consciousness and unconsciousness ideology that if we can get our enemies to love us then we can get around to loving ourselves. But as I pointed out earlier, if the enemy's status, economic, social and otherwise, relies on his cultivation and maintaining of a hatred toward us, then that enemy will never get around to loving us. If we depend upon our enemy loving us before we love ourselves, then we will never get around to loving ourselves. Consequently, we must forget about getting the enemy to love us, getting our oppressors to love us and so-call respect us. We must go directly and speak directly to our hearts, our minds, love ourselves and love each other, because it is through that love that we advance our interests.

When we look at the legacy of Marcus Garvey we see again an emphasis on productivity. Marcus Garvey did not have to read Frederic Engels, Karl Marx and Vladimir Lenin, even though he was familiar with them. He did not have to read those to recognize the intimate relationship between the means of production and the character of a people, to recognize the intimate relationship between the nature of the economic relationships of people and their social relationships one with the other. It was apparent in his observing of our people across the world. He recognized, as we must recognize, that social character is to a significant extent determined by the nature of social and labor relations. He recognized intuitively that the eating at lunch counters with our enemies, the sharing of hotels and beds with those enemies, the marrying and sleeping with their daughters, would not advance our interests ultimately as a people; that consuming their products would not rescue us from subordination. Ultimate freedom and independence is founded on production, upon the creation of employment, upon the creation of labor and the creation of products for our own consumption. When we look in the world today, we will see that the powerful nations and people are producing people, not consuming people. As I've often said, you cannot consume yourself into equality;

you cannot consume yourself into power. Those nations who depend upon consumption will see as they consume the product of others and do not produce themselves, that they will be consumed by others.

We see that happening right here in the so-called United States of America. We hear the people now in Congress and other places bellyaching about how the Japanese closed out their markets and how we cannot sell in the Japanese markets. But how did the Japanese invade this market. The economists now know that this country is living on borrowed time, that it is spending beyond its means. Its so-called Reagan prosperity is a bogus prosperity that is dependent upon the input of foreign nations. Japan, to a good extent, along with a few of other nations, is financing the consumption habits of the United States. At some point this nation is going to have a moment of truth and we, as Afrikan people, must recognize that we're going to be caught in the very jaws of that moment.[1] This kind of economic relationship cannot continue forever. We've seen evidence of it this week, where tariffs will be imposed upon Japanese products. We have seen a wholesale stripping of the United States of its industrial base. The Midwest is now called the "rust belt", because industries have literally been flown outside of the nation. There has been a reported decrease in unemployment. Yet when you look at that decrease, you see it in the so-called service areas. You see the touted increase of jobs in the areas of the McDonald's and the Bojangle's, but not in the areas of manufacture. As a matter of fact, there is a continuing decline in the area of manufacture in this country. Thus we have a superficial ideology that's built around service and service industries, but not around productivity. This white man is recognizing that in this nation he's got to do something about it or else he will fade. We as a people must recognize as well that we cannot move forward based on consumption; we must produce and out-produce our enemies. That is our ultimate salvation. No other thing will do. That was the legacy Marcus Garvey left us, and left us very strongly, the charge that we must engage in productive labor, growth and development if we are to survive, period.

Looking at these few statements in regard to the legacy of Marcus Garvey, there must be in some of your minds the questions: Did it succeed? And if so, why are we in the state we're in today? I must frankly state that I am somewhat disturbed by the fact that, to a degree, even though certainly the spirit of Marcus Garvey lives in the hearts of many of us, it has not manifested itself as much as it should have and as much as it can. As a matter of fact, when we look at our situation today we see an actual decline in black economic development, not only in this country, but in the world in general. We have been witnessing the last few years, even in this country, a backward slide in our economic and political development. What happened in terms of the legacy of Marcus Garvey? Certainly there can be many reasons for that and I'll just look at a few. One of them I believe was, and is the ascendancy of the assimilationists—the integrationists; those leaders who came and tried to project an unreal hope that we could advance the interests of our people by identifying with the destinies of our enemies; those people who tried to get us to forget our color, our Afrikan heritage, and have suppressed those of us who are trying to maintain our Afrikan identity and destiny. When you coupled that kind of leadership and a few concessions by the establishment, with a type of economic prosperity that made an appearance in the 1950s and maintained itself through the 1960s, there emerged a combination that worked against the interests of the nationalist organizations and the nationalist ideology. We saw a nationalist and neo-colonial leadership that fell for the delusions of the so-called establishment, or the system, and has misled the people into thinking that their ultimate salvation is that of identifying and becoming one with its oppressors. It is the result of a leadership that is trying to get us to accept the reality of our oppression.

Irony of Education The paradox I have to deal with daily in my classroom is the amount of lying that must take place in the name of education; the amount of outright deception that goes by the name of education; how truth must be nailed to the cross in classroom after classroom; how people tremble, quake and suffer from anxiety when truth and reality is brought up by their teachers; how people are pushed out of the universities and punished because they dare talk about truth; how people think they should go to school only to be made comfortable. I have to warn my students time and time again that when you enter my classes you are not going to be comfortable. I'm here to raise your level of anxiety and your level of fear. I am here to make you suffer because, if you are in any class, particularly a social science class and you are comfortable, chances are that you are being lied to. It is in these classes that you must attain a confrontation with yourself, with reality and where you must attain a confrontation with the lying world that has created you in terms of who and what you are now. You must confront the nature of this *beast* called *education*, of which you are a part, and how it is going to transform you into a beast; how you then must become conscious of what it is doing to you, and against you, so that you may escape its planned destiny for you.

And each day they sit in my class, Asians, whites, Afrikans, Hispanics, and ofttimes it's an exercise in twisting, turning and squirming because I dare talk about slavery, colonialism, the sickness of Europeans; the lying, deceptive and devilish nature and the pathology of the people who now rule the world; because I dare talk about the irony of where white men sit down and determine the destiny of a world that's over 90% colored; when I dare tell them that they sit in these classes and let these whites and their education brainwash and propagandize them into servitude, and how their education is an education into ignorance. But if we are to rescue our children, students and our people, these unpleasant issues must be dealt with forthrightly.

When we deal with an assimilationist leadership that sees solutions to our problems as getting our children more soundly educated in these lies, we are going to see a decline and the destruction of Afrikan people who think that their salvation is one of being educated by the very people who destroyed them in the first place. We have a paradox there. Why is it that the arbiter of truth, the validators of truth are the very people who lie to us most? I often have to remind my students and my audiences that were I to say something, you would have a hard time believing it, but if a white man comes in and says it you believe it right away. You have to be conditioned to accept truth and see truth as coming out of the mouths of these liars.

How is it that this education makes a people backwards such that the first people they believe are the people who lied to them most, that the first validators of truth are the people who have manipulated their very lives through lies and deception?[2] I've indicated time and time again how you cannot have this 10% of the world's population ruling over the other 90% unless that 10% keeps the 90% out of its mind. It can only achieve its dominance over the other 90% through deception. The very essence of the identity of

Satan, the Devil, is that he is a deceiver. The very source of his power, the very foundation of his bringing humankind down and the destroying of mankind was through the lie. We must recognize that the white man's rule depends upon ongoing deceptions and lies. Ultimately, then, we cannot see him as the foundation and basis of truth. Thus we cannot let him be the educator of our children and let the reality that he projects become our reality. For he is sick of mind and heart. He is deceived by his own lies and therefore the reality he projects must be a lying reality. He suffers and he is deadly. How can we not suffer and die if we accept what he sees as real and unreal? Those leaders who seek to tell us that we can only rescue ourselves through accepting the identity of the white man and to accept so-called reality of the white man are leaders who will lead us to our peril and our death.[3] We must recognize that if we are to live, we have to remove these kinds of leaders.

Externalized Perception A people ignorant of themselves are a people headed for disaster. One reason for the condition we're in today is a leadership that has not yet decided it will determine a new reality and develop an Afrocentric reality, one that is suitable to the advancement and development of Afrikan people. We have a leadership that has rejected and dispensed with self-knowing for knowing of the enemy. We have a people who pride in the fact that they know more about the history of their enemies than they know about themselves; who pride in getting degrees in the history of their enemies while knowing nothing about who and what they are as a people. We have a leadership that has made us think that knowledge of self was not important, that knowledge of our oppressor was the only important knowledge, that knowledge of who and what he was about is the only knowledge of importance. Consequently, the more knowledge and education these leaders gained in terms of the knowledge of the oppressor, the more ignorant they became of themselves.

THE ASSIMILATIONIST TREADMILL

The Illusion of Progress We have a leadership that has sought to get us to accept the status quo: the control of the world by the European. You errantly hear some of us conceding that it's the white man's world so we may as well learn how to live in it or just get along. The assimilationist often accepts, consciously or unconsciously, the idea that the white man will continue to rule the world. He bases his ideology and political action on the concept that somehow our destiny is not to overthrow the white man, that our destiny is not to remove this pathological person; that our destiny is not to suppress and bring these sick people under control but to heal them in some sort of way, to convert them, to even become a part of them. Our destiny becomes not one that sees the very system and very ideology upon which these oppressors move as one of sickness and insanity and therefore in need of replacement by an Afrikan-centered and healthy ideology that comes out of our own self-knowing. This leadership wants us to accept this sickness as normality and to follow these pathological beings into self-destruction.

And consequently you will see the enemy's children, the enemy's personality being held up as normal, as representing the norm. Our behavior, to the degree that it differs from that of our enemy, is seen as deviant and thus abnormal. To that degree, we confuse equality with sameness, where we think that in order to be equal or greater than our enemy we have to be the same as our enemy; to the degree we think differentness automatically represents inferiority and therefore we become alarmed at anything that says we are somehow different from our enemy. We must recognize, ladies and gentlemen, that racism is a sickness, that the exploitation and wholesale rape and pillaging of the earth by the European represents a pathology — an illness. Therefore, our destiny is *not* one of trying to become a member of this gang of thieves, but to end its existence here on earth, to inhibit its rapacious ways and to bring this group of people to heel!

Yet we have a leadership that makes us think that our only crime has been that we've been left out on the looting of these thieves. We get a leadership that cries about how we're only getting a certain percentage of their robbery and thievery. We must recognize, Afrikan people, that it is not about getting a piece of the stolen gains of these people, but to stop their thievery and rape of the world, period! So it is not about being left out of the mainstream; it is about bringing into being a new world order.

We have had a leadership, and I'm still talking about how we moved away from Garveyism, that in its ascendance could not love itself except that it was loved by whites. To a good extent, the assimilationist ideology was one as represented in their Supreme Court struggles that said black children could not love themselves until loved by white children; that the self-hatred found in black people was because their masters did not love them; that the lack of self-respect was because we were not respected by our oppressors. Therefore, we put our children into schools with whites very early in life that they might then get a chance to see that we were really human, that we were just like them, and that they could come and accept us as they accept themselves. Thus the "reasoning" that if they came to accept us as they accept themselves, then we would come to accept ourselves — a very curious and specious ideology and psychology that lays the basis for self-acceptance on the acceptance of enemies. Therefore, we've been waiting for the last two hundred years for our enemies to love us — and accept us — so that we can get around to loving and accepting ourselves.

Often I ask the question: What if they never get around to loving us; what if they never get around to accepting us? A people whose love is based upon external sources and who must get around to themselves through the love of external people, are a people who are under control of those external forces and external people; a people who have no will and destiny of their own; a people who are ultimately reactionary in nature, whose major concern is the attitude of their enemy. They are a people who are obsessed and compelled to look at and study their enemy day and night; who make a scholarship of looking at the every move of their enemy and reading every scintilla of the enemy's body language as a way of determining their own behavior. Hence, they never get around to knowing themselves, accepting and loving themselves. We have this leadership that looks at a minuscule population in the world, a 10% population, as a cue as to how they themselves should behave. It is a case of the tail wagging the dog, where a small group of people wags the rest of the world, because the dog is obsessed with trying to catch up with its tail.

This leadership has thus robbed us of the Marcus Garvey legacy. We have a leadership that has sold us conspicuous consumption as a way of salvaging our egos. It makes us think that we will be equal to the white man when we can drive the same cars, have the same jobs, sleep in the same beds and buy in the same neighborhoods — a consumer equality: not an equality of ownership; not an equality based on wealth. We've got a leadership that talks to us about "equality of income." I have often pointed out the difference between income and wealth. We will not be equal to the white man when we have equal income. You can get an income from a salary, but you can also get an income from the ownership of resources. A man can have a $1,000,000 worth of land and get an income of $10,000, and another get an income of $10,000 working for someone else. Even though they have equal incomes, they are not equally wealthy. So we have a leadership that has sold us on *income equality*, but not wealth. It's a leadership that's going to look at income instead of the ownership and control of Afrikan property and wealth, a leadership that looks at the amount of consumption as a gauge of its equality, that looks at the degree to which it can consume as much as its master as a basis of equality — not the degree to which it owns its means of production and has control over its own inherited wealth.[4]

We have had that kind of leadership and thus have seen Afrikan people the world-over — in this country and on the Afrikan continent — give up the very basic wealth of their own lands and their very basic real estate to their enemies for a few pennies and materials which fade away and are corruptible. We have a leadership that is not concerned with developing its own productive capacities, but with merely getting jobs and being *identified with* the productive capacities of others, with literally marrying the enemy and thus trying to achieve the status of the enemy through marriage instead of through strength and power.

We have seen this assimilationist leadership — which came to the fore and to a degree has pushed back the nationalist leadership — reign over the decline of Afrikan people the world-over; the decline in Afrikan education; the disruption of the Afrikan family; the retardation of Afrikan technology; the decline and paralysis of Afrikan economics; the rampaging of our community by drugs; the colonial occupation of our community by foreign police forces and others who are not members of the Afrikan community. When we look over the past 20 to 40 years, we see an assimilationist leadership that has brought us to the terrible moral, economic, social, political, and educational impasse that we are griping about today; that has made us now face the Howard Beaches and the other kinds of disasters that are occurring daily, making us see racism rear its ugly head in a very direct way on the campuses of Columbia University, University of Massachusetts at Amherst, and the University of Michigan — the so-called bastions of white liberalism. We must recognize, Brothers and Sisters, that we cannot put our faith in the goodwill of our enemy, only in our own strength and power. A leadership that depends upon converting the white man is a leadership that is placing us in a very perilous situation. It is a leadership that ultimately is placing us in a position to be destroyed.

While we may look at the assimilationist leadership, as black nationalists who carry on the legacy of Marcus Garvey *we* must also look at ourselves. While we may gloat to a degree in the failures of the assimilationist leadership and show them the squalid outcome of their leadership — how they fought for equal housing and yet now a major problem is homelessness; how they fought for integrated schools and now a major problem is dropout-ism and illiteracy; how they threw their bodies before tractors and threw their bodies before traffic to get us into the colleges and universities, yet we find now our major problem is the decline of black students on the university level, the decline of black teachers on college campuses, the decline of black teachers in the schools, period, and the decline of the education of black people as a whole; how they struggled to get a justice on the Supreme Court and how we face injustice everyday in the courts of the United States and the world-over; how they struggled to get us to have window dressing jobs and now our children and people are unemployed in the streets of our cities, how we are facing the possibility that we may have a 70% or more unemployment rate among black males in the future; how they placed their faith in the so-called law, a law which is only as good as the people who enforce it; how their faith in redeeming the white man from his pathological racism has shown that this faith is hopeless . . . – we must *also* accept our responsibility in the decline (to a degree) of our ability to carry out the Marcus Garvey legacy. How has this occurred? To a degree, *simultaneous* with the rise of assimilationist leadership, I think we had a rise of pseudo-nationalistic leadership – a nationalist rhetoric without a nationalist substance, a people who talked a good nationalism but who do not behave and actualize what that nationalism means. *We are now engaged in a struggle between true nationalism and counterfeit nationalism.* It is time for us to remove those counterfeit nationalists, who are also in a subtle sort of similar way the partners of the assimilationists.

THE TRUE NATIONALIST

The Restructuring of Garvey's Legacy Let us look again at the nationalist who is true to his cause and let us test our nationalists by some of these criteria. *The true nationalist is not obsessed with the past to the exclusion of the present.* We have some nationalists whose heads are on backwards and they can only look in the distant past. They're so concerned with the past until they stumble over the present and cannot see what is coming in the future. They grovel and revel in the great glories of the past to the absence of the future. One of the things I think you will see in the Marcus Garvey legacy is that while he raised the black man's past to great heights, projected that past and made it a part of the consciousness of black people, there was a thoroughgoing concern with the present and the future. There was a thoroughgoing concern with the constructing of the now and the future. There was not merely an ongoing, exclusive and compulsive concern with things that were, but with things as they are, with things as they can and shalt be.

The true nationalist is forward-looking and futuristic. I see too few conferences, too few people concerned with the future, even nationalists: "What is going to occur in the year 2000? What will the condition of the people be in the year 2050, 2100? What must we do today to secure the survival and the advancement of Afrikan people the world-over? What must we do to fight off the threat of the Asian takeover of the world? We are not only confronted with the white man today; we are also confronted with other people in the world. We are confronted with a rise of Asian civilization. *Are we to throw off or to see the death of European civilization, only to fall under the yoke of the Asian civilization?* We can look out in our streets today and see it coming. It is around us everywhere. The invasion of our communities by the Asian units is a sign of times to come. The Afrikan is at the crossroads today where Afrikan people must not only evoke their great past, but now they must evoke their future as well — and create that future.

The true nationalist does not escape and hide through the glorification of the past what must be done in the present and in the future. The bogus nationalist, however, rises and raises up the people, builds up a false pride in the people in terms of past history, but he leaves them groping as to what must be done now. He leaves them feeling high-

and-mighty when they walk out of the lecture halls, auditoriums and churches, with his oratory ringing in their ears — only to face the Korean stores once they get outside, only to face their communities taken over by Arabs, by Hispanics and other groups. And with that ringing oratory and rhetoric, they must face the reality that while the knowledge of history is wonderful, great, and a necessary part of our resurrection as a people, it is not going to be our sole basis of salvation. Besides concerning ourselves with our past, we must concern ourselves with now and must use now to create the future.

The true nationalist is intrepid. Not that the nationalist does not have fear, but he learns to operate *in spite of* fear; fear does not paralyze him. He uses the fear as energy to move forward and to confront his enemies. He does not hide his fear behind high-sounding phrases, high-sounding scholarship and dredging up the past. He dredges up the past as a means of integrating it into his personality, as a foundation for his movement forward and his thrust into the future. He does not put forth a kind of pseudo game, as I see many nationalistic people putting forth; a sort of participate with the establishment, sort of arouse the revolutionary fervor of their audiences, but when you stop and think about it, they have left you with no real tools and techniques for dealing with our current problems, and do not project the future and what it will be like.

The true nationalist is entrepreneurial: he's building something; he's constructing something. We see that in Garvey; not just a concern with the past, not just an identification with Egypt and other great Afrikan empires of the past, not just picking up little detail upon little detail of some Afrikan past, but of a sound movement forward in concrete, brick and mortar construction; a sound, hands-on developing and actualization of Afrikan ideology and political development. He is one who thrusts his fear aside and moves forward, the true Afrikan nationalist.

He not only respects his ethnic heritage and the glories of his ancestors, but he is equally, if not more, concerned with the inheritance he's going to pass on to his children, with the legacy he's going to give to his children. There are people who scrape their monies together, give it to the airlines, give it to the Arabs, jump out the plane, bow, scrape and kiss the earth, just to salve their own wounded egos. But when asked for that $1,500 toward the feeding of our children, toward the educating of our children, toward the creation of jobs for our people, toward the gaining of control over *real* estate and the gaining control over our wealth, somehow they're not able to make those sacrifices. They're willing to worship the pyramids of 4,000 years ago but will not build pyramids in the present so their children may see what they left behind as well.

We have then a leadership who rallies the people to look at past glories but leave their own children neglected; who will make great analytical and oratorical dissertations on the inadequacies of Eurocentric education and yet will not contribute one penny of their monies and their time to the construction of their own schools; who year after year will spend millions and give it away to the others, but will not give it to their young. That is pseudo-nationalism, ladies and gentlemen. We see the true nationalist in the guise and person of Marcus Garvey, in the person of the Honorable Elijah Muhammad, who not only complains about the nature of the education of Black children but who does something about it. He builds the schools and universities and constructs and instructs as a part of his nationalist mission. As the Bible says, "You can tell a tree by the fruit it bears." Look not only at the words, at the scholarship, at the dredging up of the past. Look at the fruits of the labors of your leaders. See what real and concrete comes from their words.

The true nationalist is not obsessed about the destruction of his civilizations, about the cruelty of his fate and the devilishness of his enemies. Certainly he analyzes that and looks at it. Certainly he laments the destruction of black civilization and the fall of our empires and kingdoms and our fall from grace to a degree. But he does not become traumatized by those falls and destruction. He does not become obsessed and compulsive about their analysis. He looks at them, he learns from them, he integrates them into his personality and ideology, he swears never again, and he moves forward using that knowledge to construct a new civilization. He looks at the mistakes of his ancestors; he looks at the mistakes of his past civilizations and he integrates those mistakes into his personality; he then moves forward to build new civilizations, new worlds, and found new empires—not just lament the ones past and gone.

He does not exclusively study his past, but seeks to study and determine the future. He opens himself up to all kinds of knowledge and information as a way of getting to know reality. He does not spend too much time sputtering in impotent rage against his oppressors — rage that does not advance his interests — but he works calmly and steadfastly to bring into being a new order. He does not indulge in ancient and esoteric ceremonies merely to salvage his wounded ego, wounded pride, and merely to divert his interests and to expend his time. He does not get carried away in moons, numbers, and so forth as a way of guiding his life. He recognizes that while he may be into phases of moons and the movements of planets, the real world moves by the operation of hand, brick and mortar being stacked one atop the other.

Though the true nationalist recognizes the greatness of Osiris [Asar], Isis [Aset] and all of the rest, he recognizes that ultimately the pyramids were built by the hands of men. I have yet to see a god build a temple. I see men building temples; I see men building cities; I see men and people digging the mines; I see people doing the jobs. While we may get into the spirit-gods and so forth — it is great that we re-evoke those gods, look at those religions, get into the ideologies, get into the astrology and get into the esoterica — ultimately, though, we must come back down to earth and deal with the real things that are happening right here. There is nothing wrong with using the astrologies, the esoteric religions and using the moons and planets as guides for our behavior; but let us not become obsessed with them to such a degree that we do nothing else. In fact, in my daily life the most retarded people I see, in terms of economic, social, political and personal development, are the ones who know the most about the moon, the most about the planets, the most about the numbers-and-you [numerology]. Ofttimes I have to remind them: When are you going to use some of this stuff for your own self-advancement? How is it that you can give all of this great and wonderful advice to everyone else but you cannot use it for yourself? Why not demonstrate the effectiveness of what you're talking about into your own behavior, life, and therefore be a beacon to other people, demonstrate through your life-behavior and habits the effectiveness of your ideologies, religions and concepts? I don't say don't believe in it; but let it work for you! Kind of reminds me of the remark that in one instance, one man's religion works for him; his religion serves him. For the man who's down and out, he serves his religion.

We have to differentiate between a religion, an ideology, and an esoteric ceremony that works for and serves us. We need to jettison a belief that requires our service and yet does not advance our interests and thus does not change our political/social situation. We've got a lot of people out here who are serving ceremonies, who are serving ideologies, but whose ceremonies and ideologies are not doing a service for them. We can differentiate between the pseudo-nationalist and the true nationalist in the question of whether his religion, his ideology, his philosophy is serving him or is he merely serving them. We must recognize that while it is fine to worship the ancients, praise and respect our ancestors, we must not become so obsessively worshipful and so obsessed about their respect that we refuse to see about our own children, that we refuse to become great ancestors in our own right, that we refuse to take care of our future.

A brief look at the movement of the Asian today. If you study a bit of Asian culture you will recognize that at its very center is so-called ancestor worship – great respect for the ancestors. At the very center is a huge and long history built around tradition. But one of the things that puzzles western man (the European) as he looks at the Asian, is how the Asian, though he respects highly his ancestors and engages in ancestor worship and is exceedingly traditional, at the same time technologically equals and advances over him. He shows very clearly that one can still respect, love and worship the ancestors yet still be very much into the world of today, can still move and advance technologically and otherwise beyond his or her enemies. The worship and respect for ancestors and the respect for tradition do not imply that we cannot concern ourselves with the immediate and with the future. The correct worship of ancestors and the correct praise of tradition is the foundation for and advancement in the future. The pseudo-nationalist engages his people in the obsessive worship and praise of ancestors to the destruction of his future concerns and that of his children.

The true nationalist not only educates the wounded egos of adults, but also educates its young. We see many of our nationalist organizations concerning themselves weekend after weekend with the education of grown people. That's fine and is a part of the education and advancement of the race. But we must recognize that we have to educate our young as well and that the true survival of the race must couple the education of the parents with the education of the children. Nationalist organizations that are concerned almost exclusively with the education of adults and not with the education of children are practicing a nationalism that is incomplete. That is why you see in Marcus Garvey and Elijah Muhammad a concurrent education of the adults and the children, an education of the family as a whole and of individuals as well. A true nationalist knows he must educate, as the word *nationalism* implies, the nation — and everyone in it.

When you see a nationalist organization only educating its adults, you may get a clue that you have an organization that may not be so concerned with the educating of people but are people who are dealing in a compensatory way with their hurt pride, people who are more concerned with salvaging their own ego pains than with really advancing the interests of their people. These are people who will often spend tons of money upon the salvaging of their own egos and yet rob their children of a sound education and development. Therefore, the true nationalist sees the education of *all* as his destiny.

The true nationalist recognizes the unity of the relationship between education and building, its interrelationship with politics, economics, and religion. He is not just a specialist. You see in the organizations of Marcus Garvey and Elijah Muhammad, not just organizations centered around some special concern, just concerned with jobs or just with the legal aspects of black people or only with the education of black people, but organizations that were concerned with all aspects that had to do with the advancement of black people. In the organizations of Marcus Garvey and Elijah Muhammad we see the advancement of a culture, not just a political ideology, but of a full culture that concerned itself with the reconstruction of the family, the education of its children, the development of an economic system — ultimately with the development of a nation and the development of a people. Therefore, the true nationalist sees a unity and a relationship between things and recognizes that all aspects important to the advancement of our people must be developed, spoken to and related one to the other. There is a unity then between economic, social and psychological development. You can't only use lectures in psychology to transform a people, neither can you use the teaching of history alone. These people must be concretely engaged in the gaining of their own freedom, the construction of their own independence, and in the building of their own fate. In fact, the best psychotherapy of all is the psychotherapy of constructing one's own civilization and fashioning one's own nation.

The true nationalist recognizes the necessity of building both a national and an international government; that we ultimately must build in this country a nation, and nations of Afrikan people the world-over. A true nationalist is not afraid to delegate power. We have a lot of people who enter into nationalism bearing their egotistical problems with them. We have a lot of people who think that because a person spouts a nationalist ideology, he or she has overcome selfishness, greed, self-centeredness, pettiness, ignorance and fear. Not hardly, ladies and gentlemen, not likely! Those things still must grow and develop. I often warn people not to fall for people merely because they project a nationalist ideology. You must look into their souls; you must look at their character and see what the character really has in it. It is that which determines your relationship with them, not just the statements of their ideology.

Ultimately if we are to control our destiny, as Marcus Garvey indicated, we must become self-governing. A nationalism not talking about self-government, not talking about nation-building, not constructing a national network, not constructing a national economic, social, and political system, is a false nationalism, Brothers and Sisters. Therefore we've had a leadership that while it has inspired us with this knowledge of history and knowledge of the past, inspired us with its daring to curse the white man out, has left us bereft of a nation, a government, a structure, and the only means by which we can defend ourselves against our enemies and thus determine our destiny. Do not then be deceived by words: we must look at deeds!

A true nationalist not only motivates through language, rhetoric and oratory, *but trains*. You cannot train a people with a two-hour lecture on Saturdays. You cannot train people with monthly or weekly meetings. I often get people who ask me, "Why do we do this? Why can't we just get it?" They throw up their hands in exasperation. "Why do we behave in this way or that way? Can't we see? What must we do in order to overcome these . . . whatever?" I get this kind of bedevilment. Often the questions are asked with the expectation that some kind of magical formula is going to be handed out. Just *abracadabra!* and things will change; just make a few passes across your heart or such and it's going to change! It's not that way. *You do what every other people have done*. What do you think these schools are out here for, Brothers and Sisters? What do you think the colleges are here for? What do you think the various institutes are here for? They are here to train people to behave the way they are expected to behave. You don't leave it to circumstance and happenstance for your people to behave the way they should behave. You *train* them to behave the way they should behave. That is why you build schools. The Japanese do not ask why don't their children behave this way: they train them to behave this way; they inculcate them and they send them to school. Once a week, two hours on Saturday? No! **Everyday!** Throughout the Summer! Every evening! They spend more time with their teachers and their trainers often than with their parents. This is what you do. If you want your people to behave *correctly* economically, then you have to educate them economically. If you want them to behave in the family sort of way, correctly, then they have to be educated to be familial. If you want them to behave correctly in terms of self-respect toward one another, then they have to be trained to behave with respect toward one another. This is not something that comes about by accident. *Institutions* have to be developed and built so that this training could take place. The greater part of their time and the time and efforts of our children should be dedicated to being trained to acquire the behavior that we need to advance our interests. We are not going to get that behavior if we depend upon that behavior being trained into our children by our enemies, by people who *need* to have ill-adjusted and maladjusted behavior to *maintain* their power position in life.

In summary, you cannot advance the interests of your people merely by talking about our greatness for a couple of hours in the afternoon. You're going to have to teach it, day in, day out, and place your students and your people in a position so that they may learn how to behave and how to resolve their problems. The intelligence, though it is something that is given, has to be shaped.

The true nationalist leader sees to the welfare of his people. When you study the history of the other groups in this country, the Japanese and the Chinese particularly saw to it that the welfare of their people was not in the hands of other people. When you read in the past where the Chinese and the Japanese were suffering greatly from economic oppression, they still did not let their people go on welfare through the general system. They built their welfare programs and their own internal caring program. They recognized that when people must beggar and be supported by their enemies, they are going to be directed by their enemies and thus their destiny is going to be determined by their enemies. Consequently, if you have a nationalist leader who is not moving and designing such that the people can care for themselves and their own interests, then you are dealing with a pseudo-nationalist – not a true nationalist.[5]

You see in Marcus Garvey a man who was building with his organization a means by which the welfare of Afrikan people could be the basis, the concern of, and be founded upon the work and activity of Afrikan people; not upon other people who have stolen our wealth in the first place and who we now have to beg for a little bit of it in the second. The true Afrikan leader, then, rewards his people. The approval of his people is the greatest approval he can gain. We still have people who gain their greatest sense of self through degrees and through the minor rewards given them by their enemies. We often honor our own people to the degree that they have been given these symbols of authority by another people. We have to recognize that the true nationalist becomes the source of his own rewards and the source of the approval of his own people. Categorically, it is the rewards and approval by our own that is the final and the ultimate reward to which they strive. It is through getting rewarded and approved in this way that we advance the interests of our people.

The true nationalist grounds his social and political philosophy and practice on a *realistic analysis* of his situation. He cognizes his enemies. He is not a slavish reader of foreign sources and of other political ideologies. He does not permit his reading of Marx, Lenin and those other people to paralyze his ability to think creatively. He understands that the ultimate foundation for political activity and behavior is his own realistic analysis for himself of his situation and his circumstances. His ultimate decisions, social, political, economic and otherwise, must be grounded on that knowledge, not upon a theoretical knowledge of people who belong to the enemy. Does it mean that he should not read the other people? Certainly he can read the other people, but his ultimate decision is based on his own analysis, upon the sound knowledge of himself, who and what he is, and upon his reality.

The true nationalist is not a purist to the degree that he is paralyzed. Some of us want to be nationalists but also want to be so pure that — in the end — we end up doing nothing. We end up paralyzed. We would go into business, but that's capitalism, isn't it? So we don't go into that. We would do this, but that's in some way related to this ideology or to that enemy ideology. So you see the individual often trying to be such a pure nationalist until he cannot engage in real, practical behavior. He is so concerned about getting his hands dirty that he dares not do anything at all. We can see the nationalist who is so hung up in his traumas of nationalism and capitalism that he dares not engage in any economic development. He sees himself as having been victimized by capitalistic greed, certainly by the European, until he becomes afraid of money. He sees himself so used and exploited for economic ends until he does not determine exactly where money and wealth fit within his social and ideological systems. Consequently, we get a nationalist who is hung up waiting for Afrikan communalism to come into being, or communism; who is also frightened to engage in any kind of business, *because that's capitalism,* so he remains frozen while the other economic groups move into his community, taking his economic resources, unemploying his children and using his wealth against him.

Deductively, the true nationalist recognizes that in this world, though we may want to be as pure as possible and may strive for perfection, it means at times we have to face reality for what it is and get out of it what we can and do the best with what we've got; not let ourselves be caught up with a puritanism that does nothing but set us up for destruction. The true nationalist is not caught up in indecisiveness and in some pie-in-the-sky dream about classless societies. He gets engaged in the true work of building and construction.

The true nationalist is also not afraid to overthrow tradition when tradition is unproductive. He is not one who just gives obeisance to Afrikan tradition out of some blind ignorance. He is one who says: "Even though I revere the Afrikan past and I revere the Afrikan tradition, that tradition can be built upon. I and my generation have something to add to that tradition. I have a right then to use the legacy of that tradition to confront the realities of my current times and thus modify that tradition and see to the survival of my people." Therefore, the true nationalist does not just manipulate and threaten with tradition but uses tradition creatively, knowing that as long as that tradition is used for the advancement of Afrikan people, then it is Afrocentric tradition.

The true nationalist is thus not afraid to engage in productive behavior. Where one sees nationalism, one sees construction, actual growth and development. Where one sees nationalism, one sees building, one sees institutional development; one sees trade, development and commerce; one sees restructuring of values, restructuring of priorities; one sees the rebuilding of relationships; one sees the reallocation of resources. When we as nationalists say that we are carrying out the legacy of Marcus Garvey, let us show that legacy in concrete development, institution building and, ultimately, nation-building.

I

Ethiopia, thou land of our fathers,
Thou land where the gods loved to be,
As storm cloud at night suddenly gathers
Our armies come rushing to thee.
We must in the fight be victorious
When swords are thrust outward to gleam;
For us will the victory be glorious
When led by the red, black and green.

Chorus

Advance, advance to victory,
Let Africa be free;
Advance to meet the foe
With the might
Of the red, the black and the green.[10]

10. The first stanza of the UNIA's national anthem known as the Universal Ethiopian Anthem.

To deny Afrika is to deny the world.

Part Two

Afrikan-Centered Consciousness, Personality and Culture as Instruments of Power

God in the affairs of men is
on the side of the strongest battalion.

✧ ✧ ✧

The white man's propaganda has made him
the master of the world, and all those who have come
in contact with it and accepted have become his slaves.

Marcus Garvey

Part Two

Thank you kindly for your warm welcome. It's great to be back here with you this evening. It's been a while. I always appreciate coming and being with you, and do appreciate your support, of course. Each time I've been here I've promised you our next publication, but it's definitely on the way. At last count Brother Sababu, my co-partner, told me we were right about 800 pages. We intend to give you some good wintertime reading.

We ought to recognize that we are as complicated as any other people and one of the things sometimes we underestimate is the degree to which we must address ourselves as a people. Too often we think that our issues can be described in twenty-five words or less. There are people who think we are a small and a small-minded people so they don't have to write sizeable materials. As other nations and other people require libraries to deal with their issues, so then do we.

The interesting thing about the upcoming book is that at over 800 pages it's basically a survey looking at various areas of life. We have entitled it *Blueprint for Black Power*. We are simply trying to lay out a blueprint, a prescriptive book. Now we are coming more and more into a prescriptive type of writing, laying out very practical steps and methods for achieving what it is we must achieve as

Afrikan people. This means we had to survey a lot of territory. We covered psychology, history, sociology, a great deal of political science, economics and related fields (anthropology and so forth) because all of these have to be combined in the process of nation-building. This is what we really have to be about — the process of building a nation. If you're not thinking in terms of nationhood, then I must say, frankly, you're not thinking seriously of being liberated. Trying to integrate and merge with our enemies is not going to solve our problems. And it's not going to happen. As a matter of fact, it is a fantasy that has kept us from taking care of business for far too long, the idea that we're going to one day be one with these people, that we're going to merge into "invisibility" with these white folks. Even if that were possible we should question our motives for wanting to do so. Why would we want to merge with the world's greatest criminals and thieves, with the people who have the worst values the world has ever known? It's amazing to hear some of our parents saying to our children "we want to be just like them." It's a joke.

It's an insult to hear former Vice President Dan Quayle or to hear President Clinton come and lecture Black folks on values. How dare we let these people into our churches to attempt to lecture us on values and such, to lecture to us about population control — another joke!

The first thing we think about when we think about population control is the overproduction of Afrikan people, so-called Third World people. We can solve the overpopulation problems quickly if we could reduce the European population drastically. Of course, as I tell you, this world has to always be backwards. The ones who need to be reduced most drastically have the world thinking the other way around.[6] A good deal of the problem sometimes is not the number of people in the world, but the number of *greedy* people in the world; one where you have an oft-referred to as *minority* of people who consume the vast majority of the world's resources. This large population they complain about could eat better if these greedy people weren't eating up everything. To have more for everybody to eat you have to get rid of the greedy ones, the ones who are overconsuming, the ones who are taking the food out of other people's mouths. Here you have a people who rob you, take everything you've got and then they say you don't have enough to support yourself. This is the kind of joke we've got going out here. We're going to come back to this issue of values.[7]

Power and Consciousness

We're going to peruse Afrikan-centered consciousness, personality and culture as instruments of power. Ultimately this is what this whole struggle is about, one of *Power!* Not one of loving one another and all the things we hear. Largely, the problems we are confronted with today as Afrikan people in America flow from our powerlessness or our inappropriate use of power. We've been made to think that to even talk about and think of power is sinful, that to pursue it is immoral and wrong. But one cannot exist without power. Without power there is no life; a battery without power is dead. You need power to act, to behave in the world, to deal with the world. Consequently, we must interpret what we are about in terms of power. We have the power, Brothers and Sisters. We have the possibilities. We just need to reorganize ourselves, reorganize our consciousness, our personality and our culture, and see them as instruments of power and use them as instruments of power to transform our situation.

The Imperative of Consciousness

We should not look at consciousness as some abstraction. As I often tell people, the most practical thing we could have is a good theory, a good concept to guide our behavior, to be used as an instrument to measure reality, as an instrument to test reality. A good theory organizes the world and organizes one's approach to the world. It permits one to be able to evaluate the world in terms of where one wants to go and what one wants to do. To be without theory is to approach the world on an *ad hoc* basis, to just meet it here and there and to not approach it in a systematic form. It is to live reactionarily, always reacting to what other people are doing, always being overwhelmed by events and overwhelmed by the future, instead of creating events and creating the future and making the future. When one has a good theory and a good concept, one is able to do just that.

Without human consciousness there is no world. It is the presence of human consciousness that brings meaning into the world. Without conscious human beings in this world, in effect, there would not be a world. We bring the world into being through our consciousness and through our consciousness create the world we live in. Out of the totality of reality our consciousness hews a world that fits itself. In other words, the kind of world you exist in reflects the kind of consciousness you have. Notice if you change your consciousness or change your values and orientation you enter into a different world; you interact with different people, people who you often didn't even know existed in the world, social situations that you might not have even recognized until you entered into a new level of consciousness. You observe people, for instance, who become addicted to crack or other mind-altering substances now enter into a whole world or social system that before they became addicted they hardly noticed; they didn't know what it was all about. They picked up new friends, new relations, entirely new ways of acting, altogether new purposes in life. They lost old friends, broke with old families. In other words, that addictive consciousness brought into the world a new foreground and put other things into the background.

Man's consciousness is a creative act and the kind of consciousness one has will determine the kind of world one creates. Consequently, when we look at the world we live in, Afrikan people, we must recognize that to a great extent it is a world of *our* own creation! It is a world generated by the kind of consciousness that we have permitted to be instilled in us as a people. We talk about the white man as having power. Recognize that power ultimately has to do with a relationship between people and that the white man's so-called power is to large degree based on the nature of the relationship he has with the black man. We empower him by the nature of our own behavior and attitudes as a people. He cannot be what he is unless we are what we are.[8]

The European is largely our creation. When we look at our behavior, we will see that to a good extent it is our behavior, our values, our consciousness, the kind of personalities we have established in ourselves — our tastes, our desires and needs — that maintain the European in his position. Let's examine the Civil Rights Movement and the apartheid system of the South. When blacks decided just to get out of the buses and walk, the system changed. When they just stopped sitting behind the white driver, just changing that relationship changed the nature of power in that system. When they decided to walk side-by-side, when they decided to walk abreast and ally themselves collectively, the relationship changed. They had not aligned that way before. When they kept their monies in their pockets, sat on those stools and blocked the other people from them and changed the nature of the interactions between themselves and whites, the nature of the system changed. Therefore, we have tremendous power. It depends upon how we align ourselves as a people and how we decide to relate to other people in the world. They cannot have what they have unless we are who we are. That is why we don't have to spend a great deal of time always appealing to them and analyzing them. We can better appeal to our sense of self and our own consciousness. We waste a lot of time trying to transform them when through transforming ourselves they will be transformed automatically. The power is in our hands.

Blacks as Jobs Creators

We are not destined to be the servants of white folks. That is not the destiny of black folks. We have to change this idea. Many of us are still operating on that concept. Many of us go to these schools to become qualified, to work for whites. Why do we assume that they are going to have jobs for us? These people are having difficulty making jobs for themselves. The greatest problem the Europeans are facing today and the European economies are facing today is that they are not generating enough jobs for their own people.[9] Even though the United States is bragging about the millions of jobs it is creating, the bulk of those jobs are part-time jobs, low-wage jobs, and jobs that have little or no future. So when people talk about creating jobs, you've got to ask what kinds of jobs are being created. That is why, of course, the system is not investing in black education. It no longer needs black people to maintain its employment structure. You see it bringing in people from outside of the nation to be employed. You see it even is hiring in the world itself, in other nations and other places. Already it has reached the point where its need for black males is pretty much saturated and it literally is warehousing us in the jails and the prisons and provoking us to kill each other and destroy each other out here in these streets. Yet we are still organizing the education of our children as if the white man still has jobs waiting for them in multitudes.

How different our education would be if we sent our children to school to create jobs for themselves, to create their own economic and political systems, to see themselves as the major source of their own employment. Earlier today I heard something about some people out here protesting for jobs and pushing these other people for jobs. I asked the question: Do we know how many jobs we really create for other people? We are a job-creating people. We don't realize it because we don't think in terms of nation. If we saw ourselves as a nation, we could see that we create jobs like any other nation. Look at how many jobs are created by black music? Look at the whole structure of the music industry, from promoters to manufacturers of records and tapes, to a whole entertainment field, to the sellers of music in the stores, the Tower Records and other great sellers of records, CDs, videos etc., advertising that uses our music and so forth. How many thousands of jobs are we creating as people? We are creating them, but they have them. We sing the music; they sell it. We sing the music; they market it. We sing the music; they promote it; they produce great conglomerates like SONY/CBS Music, creating all kinds of jobs. We are creating tremendous jobs for lots of other people.

How many jobs do we create just buying from Koreans, buying from other ethnic groups out here? How many people are we creating employment for in terms of our spending and our consumption habits as a people? How many jobs are we creating going to jail? We are creating all kind of jobs and wealth and we must come to understand this. We are creating these jobs and yet we are begging for jobs. *This means that somewhere our consciousness has been impaired.* We are begging for what we are making already. We cannot use our own creation as a source of our own wealth.

Black Wealth Expropriated

The Creator could not have intended for us, as Afrikan people, to be a poor people if the Creator implanted in our soils such wealth as was planted there. We talk about the minerals, the oils, gold, copper, bauxite, manganese, precious stones and that which has been implanted in Afrikan soil. So it seems that the Creator blessed us from the very beginning with wealth and possibility. Therefore, for us to be going hungry over this wealth, starving in the midst of it, to be perceived as a dependent indebted people while our wealth is being shipped out to other people — we're actually selling a lot of it for pennies, nickels, dimes and less — it means that there is something wrong with our consciousness. Ultimately, the wealth of a people is not in their land; it's in the mind. The wealth of Man is in his mind, in his consciousness.

We mentioned the example of Japan. No mineral wealth to speak of whatsoever, nothing at all. A nation, by the way, which is totally dependent. Of course we get things backwards, don't we? We see ourselves as depending on Europeans when the reality is the other way around; they depend on us, on our soil and on our people. We have to be backwards in order for this situation to be the way it is. Our reality has to be turned backwards and we have to live in almost a permanent state of deception in order to be used the way we are used. The Japanese must depend on others for their vital resources. Those products they use to create their technology and so forth are taken from the soils of other people and then sold right back to them. Yet they are seen as rich and powerful, and the people whose wealth they take or buy are seen as poor and poverty-stricken. Ultimately, then, you cannot rob or take wealth from a poor people. You cannot extract wealth from a poverty-stricken people. People who have nothing, you can get nothing from. So if you're getting all your diamonds, gold, magnesium and all this other stuff from Afrikan people, then Afrikan people must be wealthy. Therefore, if Afrikan people are poverty-stricken with this material wealth, then it must be because our consciousness as a people is impoverished and we are suffering an impoverishment of our mentality.

As we have said before, if you have a good mind you can con another joker out of his land, you can con him out of his diamonds and his gold. This is what the other people have done. They have used their minds and their cleverness to take from us what they did not have originally. Therefore, consciousness is not an abstract concept. It is not just a theoretical concept. It is a concept that is directly related to the reality that one lives in and to the reality that one experiences. It is directly related to the type of life one will live and does live. So I'm going to look at this for a minute, particularly the consciousness of Afrikans in America.

Denial of Slave Consciousness

I'm often somewhat amused and taken aback by the number of people in this society who claim that slavery occurred somewhere back there. You've got some so-called black conservatives who claim that slavery no longer influences the nature of Afrikan people. I wonder what those people have to conserve in the first place! Are they conserving power? Are they conserving wealth? What does a black conservative conserve? They've got to conserve something. And since they have very little, if anything, they must only be conserving the system that has created their poverty to begin with. And you see them ultimately justifying the poverty of Afrikan people and justifying the political, social and economic subordination of Afrikan people in the name of some kind of manufactured higher principles.

So the experience of slavery is not supposed to be operating in the mentality of black folks and you'll hear a lot of our youngsters say that as well. "Why do you talk about slavery? That was back there." Or you'll hear whites offer, "Well, we don't have anything to do with that any more." It's an amazing situation because you have to remind them: "You are still living off the interest of the wealth that your forefathers earned from slavery. You are still enjoying the accumulated wealth that began with the enslavement of our people. If you're going to enjoy the wealth that was generated by evil, then you must take the curse that comes along with it. Therefore, even though you personally had nothing to do with it, because you have received stolen goods you must pay the price as well. And because you fight and struggle to protect those stolen goods and you defend them and organize your society and our relationship to white people to maintain them and to continue to enhance them, then you must pay the price. That's why you live in terror; that's why you are stabbed in these streets; that's why you're going to suffer, no matter how "good" you are, no matter how "liberal" you are. Ladies and gentlemen, when we behave as adults we must recognize that our behavior will be visited upon our children and that our children will pay for our misbehavior. As we say and act does not end at the point of its occurrence; it continues to reverberate into the future and down across the generations. That's why when you behave in a particular way you have to think in terms of seven generations from your behavior as to how what you're going to do is going to affect those generations later on. Even though those children may appear to be so-called innocent, they will still pay the price of their parental misbehavior. This country, whose parents and whose adults have misspent its treasure and while they have enjoyed that treasure, ultimately their children will have to pay the taxes and have to pay the price. So we have a bunch of people out here who think they can rape and rob the world, think that they can enslave the world, then delude themselves that they're going to sleep well at night. It doesn't work that way.

So we have some of our people who think that slavery was back then and has nothing to do with them. Brothers and Sisters, we have never escaped slavery. We still share the slave consciousness of our great-great grandparents. We are of the same mind (to a great extent) that they were. We have not advanced beyond these people. To explain this I generally ask a series of questions. You say that slavery has nothing to do with you and slavery was back there, I ask you then: What language do you speak? When did you learn that language? Was that the language Afrikan people were speaking when taken into slavery in the Caribbean and the Americas? In other words, the language we speak at this moment *is* the slave language, the language that our slave ancestors were forced to learn. We still speak it and you can still hear the pidgin, the creole and the other carryovers in our language right at this moment, the experience that they had to go through. That language, with its words defined by history and by an experience, is the language we use to guide our behavior. It's the language we use today to talk to ourselves. It's the language we use today to learn about ourselves and to learn about the world. It's the language we use today to understand ourselves. Is there any wonder then that we are still confused? So we have not escaped slavery. We are still using a slave language and we speak the language of slaves. What kind of food do you eat? You say soul food. Was that the food of Afrikan people? Slave food, the food that we find most satisfying, the food that we find sticks to our ribs, the food we call "down home", the food that we learned to eat in the slave quarters and yet we dare say that we have escaped slavery, that we have nothing to do with "those people back there." "That was back there," we proclaim, yet our entire life and social relationships, our very definition of ourselves as a people, our very attempt to commune with ourselves is mediated by the food of slaves! Understand what I'm trying to get at? Then how can you say that you exist in another consciousness from those people?

What kind of uniforms are we wearing? What kind of clothes are we wearing? Were these the clothes of Afrikan people? This is what we've got to look at. Yes, what is this then to say that we've escaped slavery?

What kind of names do we respond to? Tamika and all these other names we've got going on out here. What kind of names do we identify with? Why is it that Afrikan names sound strange to us as a people and yet we dare say that we have a different consciousness from our slave great-grandparents? How can we say that? We are still of the same consciousness; we are still in the same position because we are still servants of the white man. *Our reason for being in America is to serve white folk and to generate wealth for them.*

There has been *no* change at all in terms of our relationship to these people.

The values that we pursue are slave values —and the values of servants. The social relations that we create and interact with were built and developed during the periods of slavery. We have not escaped it at all. It is time for us to change the slave consciousness, this consciousness of servitude that is still too much with us today.

Ultimately, I ask the question that's closest to home for a lot of our people who claim that we have escaped slavery and that slavery was something back then which has nothing to with us today. I ask you: "*What kind of god do you worship?* What's the name of it? *Who taught you to praise him?* Was this the god you were praying to *before* you were brought to these shores? Is this the religion you had before you were brought to these shores? Can you name one Afrikan god? How can you then define yourself — the very essence of yourself, the very essence of your soul — and organize the very nature of your life here on earth based on a god handed to us by our slavemasters and claim that you have no slave consciousness and are not related to slavery?"[10] In other words, ladies and gentlemen, we are not Afrikans: *We are possessed by spirits and demons!* We have let another people's spirit take possession of our bodies and take possession of our minds. When we speak, it is not with our Afrikan voice, it is with the voice of that demonic presence that uses our lips to speak its own language. Yes, we have to recognize this. We are possessed. If we are to transform ourselves and to transform the nature of our relationship with those who are our masters, we must engage in an exorcism and thus clear the devils out of our minds. And you have to be demonically possessed because, if we talk about black-on-black violence, self-defeating behavior, self-destructive behavior, then we could not be possessed by a beautiful and wonderful god: We must be possessed by a demon.

Demonic Possession

Somnambulistic Possession At this time it is worthwhile to read a bit about demonic possession. It's interesting to look at the literature on possession. We have a couple types of possession. One is called a somnambulistic possession. *Somnus* in this instance having to do with sleep; you hear it in the brand name "sominex". *Ambulistic,* to move around, ambulatory. So we're talking about people who are sleep-walking. They're not awake but they're walking around. The body is moving, it is walking in an organized fashion and walking systematically but the person is still asleep. In somnambulistic possession, the individual's original self has been repressed and displaced and he identifies with the spirit that possesses him. His eye and the spirit's eye are one and the same. We have a lot of that here today where the spirit that has been implanted in us, we have taken to be us and we've identified with it. This is why in defending ourselves we end up defending the people who rule over us. In defending our ego, we end up maintaining the social structure which has destroyed our ego to begin with. You see it in our youngsters who will fight and kill in the name of respect and fight because their egotistic orientation has been insulted. Therefore, in defending their ego they do not kill who destroyed their ego — they kill each other and maintain the ones who destroyed them in the first place in power. That's why the subtitle of my book *Black-on-Black Violence* was *Black Self-Annihilation in Service of White Domination*. We are killing each other in order to maintain this system. We have let ourselves become possessed by a spirit such that when we become aggressive, we aggress against the self instead of at those who are the source of our aggressive orientation.

Self-Hatred as a White Defense Mechanism Self-hatred is a personality configuration. It is a form of personality organization. It is an orientation toward the world and toward one's self. Self-hatred, then, is the white man's greatest protection against being destroyed by the black man. To a good extent self-hatred is the white man's defense mechanism, the white man's form of self-defense. How can we say that? To a great extent, one function of the personality is to direct energy, to direct aggression, to channel aggression, energy, wishes and impulses in particular directions, to organize feelings, to organize energy to achieve certain ends. Those things that we hate often when we are angry or hostile, we aggress against them; we often attack them; we destroy them. We have a problem then, don't we? If we attack the things we hate, if we attack the things toward which we hold hostility when we are overly frustrated and when we are angry, then what happens if that thing which we hate is ourselves? It means that when we become frustrated and angered, when we are overwrought by feelings of hostility and our self-hating personality seeks to channel that hostility and that aggression, it's going to channel the aggression right back onto the self because that's the thing we hate most. Consequently, black anger becomes a conduit for black self-destruction, for black self-defeat. The object of our hostile, aggressive feelings becomes ourselves. You can see then how the white man is protected by that personality structure. While he stokes our anger; while he stokes our hostility; while he stokes our frustration; while we get mad and want to strike out; when we decide to strike out and aggress we strike out and aggress against the self. By doing so he, the white man, is left untouched and unscathed. Therefore, our self-hatred becomes his principal means of defending himself and of maintaining himself. One of the things that frightened him most about the Colin Ferguson case was that Ferguson's self-hatred mechanism broke down! Unlike many deaf, dumb and blind "negroes," he knew who his enemies were. So when he got angry and hostile, instead of going out to drink himself to death, instead of going out to smoke crack and destroy himself, instead of going out to kill someone who looked like himself, instead of going out to commit suicide and put himself in a place to be destroyed by somebody else, he went directly to the source of his frustration. This is what frightened those people. They were wondering how many more are there like that and are their numbers increasing.[11]

You can thus see why the seed of self-hatred is planted in the minds of the black man. We spend a lot of time looking at what it does to us, but we've got to look at it from another angle. As I've told you before, every maladapted characteristic in the black psyche is there for white folk. It's not purely there because they hate you, or they misunderstand you, or they don't know who you are; it has nothing to do with all of that. When you analyze the so-called aberrations in the black personality, you must always ask the questions: What are their social functions and roles? Who benefits from this aberration in the black man's mind? What are the social, political and economic benefits, and for whom? Who gains from this particular orientation in our minds? Then you begin to see why it's there and what its function is. Thus every complaint we have about ourselves has a political, economic and social intent beneficial to white folk and detrimental to ourselves. Somewhere along the way we became possessed by these orientations and they were implanted in our personality.

We have come to identify with them as our "natural" selves, as our "natural" orientation. We have assumed that they represent who we are and we have now found many ingenious ways to defend the demons that possess us. And ultimately those demons destroy us and have us destroy others like ourselves.

Lucid Possession There's another form of possession we call *lucid possession*. In this case the person at least has a sense of self and they have the sense that there's another spirit in them and they struggle with that spirit, sometimes losing the battle. They become obsessed in their struggle with their spirit, and in a sense are disenabled by that struggle. So some of us are in that state where we're not quite satisfied with the identity we have; we know somehow that there is a deeper Afrikan self in us. We are also aware that there's a *euro*centrically implanted demon in us and we wrestle with it daily.[12]

Spontaneous and Artificial Possession There's another type of possession we talk about here and that is *spontaneous* possession, one that has sort of occurred spontaneously against our will. This is in contrast to one we refer to as *artificial,* one deliberately created. What do we mean by that? When we go into a particular social setting such as a church or a rock concert or the like, and we go through a set of rituals and behavior, we go there and go through these behaviors, rituals, songs and dance as a means of deliberately being possessed by the spirit and having our bodies taken over and being possessed. And then we say we *feel* the spirit; we feel the spirit living within us. Consequently, much of our life is about provoking – through artificial means – spirits which take over us and assume control of our behavior.

Latent Possession When we are possessed and we do not even know we are possessed, this is referred to as *latent possession*. I think that defines a lot of us. We are not even aware, and those are the hardest ones to break through because they don't sense any kind of split within the personality. They and their possessing spirit are one and the same. When you try to exorcize their possessive spirit, they feel as if you are attacking them personally. In defending their person, they defend the spirit that possesses them.

Let's be a little more concrete and I want to just give you an example of what I mean by this. In the literature we talk about these spirits which are called the *incubi* and *succubi*: a spirit that lies in the body or on the body, the *incubus*, and the one that lies under the spirit, the *succubus*. When we talk about this spirit that possesses us; when we talk about this spirit that the European implanted in us —in terms of the language, in terms of the food, the religion, the values, the social relations, the name — we are talking about a spirit that's just not a spookish entity in our selves. It actually incarnates in us. What do we mean when we talk about incarnation? We are dealing with the Latin root *carnes* which has to do with meat, flesh. In other words, the spirit comes to dwell in our very flesh and comes to sculpt our very bodies. Therefore, the spirit is a physical thing as much as it is a psychological thing. The bodies that we have tonight, ladies and gentlemen, are bodies that have been created by the European experience and are not our natural bodies as Afrikan people. Just as the surface of our bodies reflects the influence of another people, the very internal nature and the physiology of our bodies reflect those people as well. That's why when you get rid of them you're going to have a healing experience and your whole body will change.

The Multiple Personality and Enslaved Afrikans This is most dramatic when we study the so-called multiple personality. Though I have read some of this before, just indulge me again in this context. I'll read to you the description that was printed in the *New York Times*. It begins:

> When Timmy drinks orange juice, he has no problem. But Timmy is just one of close to a dozen personalities who alternate control over a patient with multiple personality disorder. And if those other personalities drink orange juice the result is a case of hives.[13]

What are we saying here? We've got one body, but depending on what consciousness possesses that body it will react to the drinking of orange juice with or without hives; it will break out in blisters. So, to drink orange juice when one of the other personalities is possessing it, welts and hives will break out right there. If Timmy comes back, if the "new" consciousness comes back and takes over that body, the hives will disappear almost on the moment. In other words then, there's a different body for a different consciousness. It goes on to say that medical disorders are found to differ from one sub-personality to another. In other words, even though these so-called personalities possess the same so-called body, each personality has a different order of illnesses associated with it. Each personality is vulnerable to a particular type of ailment, one way or the other. So what are we getting at? We are saying that each consciousness — which is represented by each personality — creates its own body, creates its own physiology and thereby creates its own vulnerability to various ailments and so forth. You have people in medical school who try to teach you that disease is a result of some kind of viral syndrome or some kind of entry into the body of some bacteria. Certainly that is a part of it. Certainly there is reality there. But the body must interact with the virus and the disease entity. This is what we mean when we talk about the immune system, that health is not necessarily the absence of the disease but is the capacity of the body to resist disease, to stand up against disease. Consequently, when these bodies are taken over by different personalities, these personalities apparently change the nature of the immune system of those bodies, making them vulnerable to diseases when one personality is present and not so when another is present. Which means, ladies and gentlemen, that the nature of the consciousness which possesses us as persons will to a degree determine the illnesses to which we are vulnerable as a person and as people.

A lot of the illnesses, physical and other diseases that we suffer from are thus mediated by the nature of the consciousness we have permitted to possess us as a people. So, to a great extent the defeat of disease – the maintaining of health – must not only be pursued in terms of discovering new drugs and such things but must involve self-discovery and self-knowledge. It goes on to state that, "In people with multiple personalities there is a strong psychological separation between each subpersonality, each will have his own name and age." Does that strike a bell? What did we say earlier? To what names do we respond? Are they the same names to which we responded prior to slavery? In other words, as we got the new slave personality we got new names . . . and we were changed. To a good extent our names were given to us to designate our *new* consciousness and our *new* situation. "Each will have his own name and age and often some specific memories and abilities."[14]

In other words, each personality has its own history, has its own biography, has its own memory. Just look at "negroes" when they have a certain consciousness and look at the history they remember. Look at the things they keep in their memories and look at the histories they study and identify with. Look at them fight Afrikan history. Look at them wanting to identify with the history of Europeans. Look at them wanting to define themselves in terms of that history and look at them having memory only for that history. Look at those Afrikans who are still under the possessive influence of the European implanted spirit and know that they have little or no knowledge of Afrikan history and therefore little or no knowledge of their own history as a person and as an individual. So there's a consistency between the consciousness and the history that a person has and the memory that an individual has.[15]

> Frequently, for example, personalities differ in handwriting, artistic talent, or even in knowledge of foreign languages.[16]

They speak a different language depending on the personality that's in there.

> Multiple personalities typically develop in people who were severely and repeatedly abused as children, apparently as a means to protect themselves against the pain of abuse.[17]

Does that strike another note in you? The *Times* continues:

> Often only one or two of the subpersonalities will be conscious of the abuse while the others will have no memory or experience of the pain.

To a great extent the personality of the Afrikan American today has been shaped by desires to escape the memory of the slave experience, to deny its existence. We don't want to talk about it; we don't want to come to terms with it; we don't want to re-experience it psychologically; we don't want to know about it. Therefore our lives become defined by eternal escape and avoidance of reality, history, and of a knowledge of who we are and how we came to be who and what we are. Consequently, we cannot act upon the reality of our history and guide our behavior and define it in terms of a fantasy of history and a misinterpretation of reality.

How did we get this religion we talked about earlier? I previously mentioned Star Trek, the time-warp that Star Trek depicts quite frequently of how people move from one state of consciousness and one world, then are suddenly flipped into a new world. They go through a warp and all of sudden everything they formerly used to guide themselves no longer counts. The language they used to speak can no longer be understood in the new world. The values they previously used to guide their behavior are no longer workable; in fact it gets them into trouble. The gods, the culture, the nature of the social relations and all of the things that they used prior to meeting the warp no longer suffice. Now they must learn new values, new behaviors and new orientations in order to adapt themselves to the new universe that they live in. We are in that kind of position today.

Consider the Afrikan and the world the Afrikan lived in prior to being brought across the ocean. Think about the gods we praised. Think about the organization of our society. Think about the languages we spoke, the food we ate, the dress we wore, the music, the songs, the dance and all of the things that defined us as Afrikan people. Think how horrendous it must have been for us to be thrown into a world where there was a whole new language, a whole new social hierarchy, a whole new set of authority – people pushing you around who you don't understand, people who are putting strange tools in your hands, people who are trying to get you to relate to them and to relate to each other in a very different kind of way from what you are accustomed. Think about the stress and the confusion and think about the abuse. Think about the horror of that situation our parents and great-grandparents were put in. And then there was someone who said, "If you pray to this god, if you talk this way, if you dress this way, if you relate this way you will get a greater sense of security. Your anxiety will be reduced; you will feel good and you will be able to withstand the pain of your existence. The god I'm going to hand you is one that I have created for you and the theology that comes with it is one that I have created so that you will continue to serve me as you continue to serve it."

We have come to believe in the veracity of that god and that religion. Why? Because we feel so secure when we follow it and we feel so relieved as we follow it. Yet we wonder why, despite all of our prayers, despite all of our devotion, we still suffer the way we do? I often ask the question: Why is it that the people who pray the most have the larger numbers of their children in the jails of America today? We who shout and kick over the benches and so forth, yet are filling up the prisons, our children killing each other and becoming addicted out here in these streets! There must be a problem here, ladies and gentlemen. We must re-orient ourselves to our religion; we must re-orient ourselves to our gods. Apparently we do not have the appropriate orientation, because as that book you read says: "You can tell a tree by the fruit it bears"! Therefore, if it bears bitter fruit or if it bears no fruit at all, the god you worship says, "It is but fit to be hewn down and thrown into the flames and consumed." Read your own bible! It gives you a very practical measure as to whether the religion you are pursuing is an appropriate one. That measure exhorts us to look at the fruit that it bears. If the kind of religion and the god you're pursuing end up having your sons in the jails of America and end up maintaining Afrikan people in slavery and servitude in their own lands and everywhere, then something is wrong in terms of how we relate to that religion – and that god – since the outcome is wrong and destructive.[18] All because we don't want to confront the abuse that we went through and deal with it.

When you go through that time-warp the only way you can ultimately come to understand the new world is to understand what happened when you went through that warp which transformed the personality, and that which made the personality what it was originally. I find that interesting when I read here what happens when the personality moves from one personality to another, when the body is possessed by one personality and that personality displaced and another one comes in.

> During the switch there is typically a period of seconds or even minutes when heart rate, breath rate and other physiological markers show a disorganization that is followed by a new pattern typical of the personality that is emerging.[19]

In other words, we go through a period of disorganization and stress and then the personalities reorganize to fit into the new circumstances. We can't continue to pursue this but it's interesting to look at the changes in blood pressure that each personality brings about and the many physical changes that are representative of the personality. What we are saying here is that each personality has its own name, its own history, its own memory, biography, way of speaking, language, way of thinking, way of perceiving itself, its own vulnerabilities. Each personality generates its own life-space and generates its own type of social relations. Each personality has its own tastes and appetites and its own morality. To a great extent, if we look at the problems and issues that confront us today as Afrikan people and see those issues in terms of the consciousness, we would recognize we must rid ourselves of the consciousness that has been implanted in us by our European masters.

One other thing I want to bring to light relative to this situation of multiple personality. When you engage people in behavior therapy and you scan their brain to look at how their brain metabolizes energy, you notice there is a relationship between the areas of the brain that are rapidly using energy, the type of mental activity a person is undergoing, and the type of physical behavioral activity the person is undergoing. Each personality, each type of orientation has a blueprint in the brain in terms of the various areas of the brain that are functionally relating one to the other. It is of interest to note, for instance, something called the *obsessive-compulsive personality* — the person who cannot stop repeating a particular behavior no matter how irrational it may be; the person who must wash their hands every thirty minutes even if they are not dirty, but who are compelled to the point that they wash their hands to rawness, because they cannot stop; the person who is absorbed by a particular type of image, by particular kinds of thought or orientation that they cannot get out of their minds. This is what we mean when we talk about the obsessive-compulsive personality, a rigid, repetitive personality. We note that if you scan the brain of these personalities, certain areas in their brain are intensely active. For example, we talked about their frontal lobes, the so-called orbital lobe of the brain, the orbital cortex of the brain — the part of the cortex that is above the eyes, the part of the cortex that concerns itself with intentionality, purpose, direction and motivation — and the connection of that cortex to the lower brain, to what we call the *cordate nucleus*, that part of the brain that deals with repetitive behavior, that deals with modulating behavior, that deals with (in its connection with the hypothalamus and the thalamus) the distribution of the senses and with organizing the senses. When we look at the compulsive personality we notice that these areas are intensely active, and active in a way that they maintain the symptoms of that personality. It has been shown that when these people take a drug such as Prozac — and they respond to it in a way that their symptoms are relieved — the intensity of interaction between these three brain areas is decreased or de-linked.

It has also been noted that you can put these same types of people through behavior therapy; that by changing the nature of the social relationship between the therapist and the patient — changing the nature of the reward and punishment that the patient undergoes in an effort to change the patient's behavior, changing the way the patient *thinks* about what is in his mind, thinks about the problems that he's in — when you can successfully reduce the symptoms of the compulsive disorder through this social conditioning, we note, too, the same kinds of physiological brain changes that occur with the intake of the drugs occur with the intake of social training. We are saying ultimately that the nature of the consciousness and the nature of the experience of the individual physically transforms the brain and physically transforms the way the brain operates. Therefore, when we talk about consciousness we are talking about something that is real; we are talking about something that transforms both the psyche and the body.

One of the things you note when the individual is possessed is that the facial muscles change and the body itself changes in a way that it literally incarnates and represents the nature of the spirit possessing the individual. To a good extent, if you're in certain religions you can tell what particular spirit is possessing the person by the very nature of the behavior that the individual is exhibiting and the very shape of their very physiological body and face. In other words, ladies and gentlemen, once we get rid of the spirits of these demons that the Europeans have implanted in our bodies, our very faces and bodies themselves will be transformed. A lot of the ways we look and a lot of the ways we organize ourselves physically is a result of the type of consciousness we have.

Culture, Consciousness, and Possession

The kind of consciousness that inhabits us largely reflects the nature of culture we live in, the nature of the culture we are a part of. Recognize, ladies and gentlemen, that culture cannot exist outside of our minds and of our bodies. Culture does not exist out there. History does not exist out there. History and culture can only exist in the minds and bodies of people. If there were no people in the world, there would be no history in the world, no culture in the world. Culture does not stand outside and direct us; it is inside of us and it directs us from the inside. Culture is instilled in our bodies and in our minds. We have to keep that in mind because sometimes we tend to see it as something separate from ourselves.

Culture indwells in us and it inhabits our bodies. Our history dwells in us and it inhabits our bodies. We reflect our history and we reproduce our history when that history becomes a part of us and is one with us. We tend to see culture in terms of music, in terms of the kind of dance we have, in terms of the songs we sing. That is a part of culture. Culture is deeper than that, however. Culture is a way of thinking. Ultimately, culture is a conspiracy. It is a means by which a group of people organizes the way they think, organizes the way they believe, organizes the way they see the world so as to create a consciousness by which they can cooperate in achieving certain ends such that they can mutually aid each other and gain ends they cannot gain as separate individuals.[20] Thus, culture is an instrument of power.

The individual through culture extends his power and the culture extends the power of the group. When we talk about music, song and dance, what we are talking is how culture ultimately comes to be implanted in our bodies. We tend to look at song, dance and music as entertainment. This is our serious mistake. We have a lot of our youth out there looking at music as mere entertainment. When we say that we are being enculturated, it means that a spirit is being implanted in us by the culture. It means our group is instilling in our bodies and in our minds a possessing spirit such that when our culture calls our name we respond to it. When our culture is in need of defense and support, we then defend it and support it because we are at one with it. In other words, why does the black man respond to the white man? Why does the black serve the white man? Why does everything that black men do benefit the white man? Why does the black man say that freedom is doing what I want to do? Why is it that everything he wants to do enriches the European? Why is it that as our youth proclaim they are free, that they are doing what they want to do and they are expressing themselves, that it involves buying a $100 pair of sneakers from white folks? Why? *Because the spirit that is implanted in the human mind and human psyche is there only to respond to its creator and to its master.* Therefore, when you let another people generate a spirit in you; when you let another people generate certain values in you; when you let another people generate a certain reality for you; when you let another people let you see yourself and see your own people in a particular sort of way, they have implanted a spirit – and that spirit has been created by and for them and only responds to them. It only responds to them in terms of furthering their interests and working against the interests of the body it possesses. This is why there's that self-destructive spirit in us.

The demon that possesses a body is not there for that body. *It is there for the creator that placed it there,* and if necessary to obey its creator it destroy that body, it will destroy that body which it inhabits. The tastes which that spirit has will be tastes that can only be satisfied by buying from its master creator. The values which that spirit wishes to satisfy and realize can only be realized by going through the aegis of the master that created it. That is why every value and every taste, every desire and every need that provokes us, every one of these things that we seek to desire, ends up having us going through white folks. And that's why we think we need them. Hence every time we satisfy them, they in someway benefit in our seeking satisfaction – because the demon that we call *ourselves* is answering to the call of its master.

Culture as Social Engineering/Entertainment Vehicle

A culture creates its own possessing spirits and enculturates and inculcates those spirits into the bodies of its members so that those members, in defending their own egos, in defending their own interests, in defending what they perceive as their own needs, in satisfying their own tastes, in satisfying their own values, satisfy the needs of the culture, enrich the culture, empower the culture, defend the culture, and advance the interests of the culture. How then does the culture implant its spirit into its members?[21] It does so in a very strong and primordial way. It uses vehicles. One of the major vehicles it uses is music. Rhythm, song, dance. A culture involves people moving together, in tandem, in rhythm. It involves them having the same temporal sense, the same kind of time clock so that they can move in synchrony one with the other. And music is about synchrony, poetry is about synchrony, song is about synchrony. Music is about symbols and ultimately it is through symbols that you evoke behavior from people. So when a culture creates symbols, those symbols are designed to evoke particular types of reactions, feelings and moods in its members. A culture establishes the potency of those symbols through rituals, through song and through dance.[22]

One of the best ways to inculcate cultural values, a cultural spirit, is through entertainment. It's while the members are being entertained, while they are feeling good, that the song is carrying the cultural values into the mind and into the body. The lyrics that represent the cultural interests and the cultural values are being carried on the vehicle of the music, carried through the vehicle of the poetry. The togetherness, the cooperativeness, the mutual movement together and the synchrony of the culture is being entrained through the music and through the rhythm of the dance. Therefore when you let another people take over your music, when you let another people take over your dance and attach their content to it, they will use your own music, your own dance, your rap lyrics, your poetry and your own cultural symbols to carry their message into your bodies and into your minds such that you can only respond to their beck and call and to their wishes. As a consequence they get you to buy those sneakers and other items by associating them with your music, with your poetry, with your rhythms, with your cultural symbols.

So they attach their content to our rhythm, their content to our songs. In this way they take our own instruments and turn them against the self. Notice how quickly when one of our youngsters [Ice-T] was rhyming "Kill the Police" that kind of content was washed right out, immediately. But what wash-out occurs when they talk about shooting each other with their glocks and the other weapons, when their contents of self-destructiveness ride on the rhythm of their song and dance and the symbols are loaded with self-destructive elements and content? What we are saying is that enculturation is a process of building in responsivity and ultimately, *respons-i-bility* —the ability to respond to a particular call. We then have appropriately enculturated ourselves when we can respond to our own culture, to our own values and to our own needs.

Culture, Personality, and Individuality

We have to look at personality in this light as well. We think our personality is ours. We must however recognize that the human being is a social animal. We exist in society; we exist in groups; we are born dependent, not independent. We have long periods of dependency and it is the social relationship between our mothers, ourselves and our group that protects us during our long periods of dependency. In a sense, we never quite get over our need for each another, our interdependency. Consequently, we are social animals and we must then respond to social situations. That they may be our personalties does not mean that they are not inculcated with a social spirit and they are not designed for a social end. In other words, the individual exists for the social unit, not for himself.

We often see individuality as something that is just for ourselves. Why are we individuals? We are individuals, to a great extent, because when our culture and group confront problems, we want to maximize the possibility that we will solve those problems by the fact that different individuals look at those problems in different ways and can contribute to the group particular perspectives which can be used as means of solving the problem for the group. So even individuals are there to strengthen the group. If all the people in the society thought and saw the world just alike, if they thought no differently one from the other, the society would be soon defeated because it would be uncreative. It would not be innovative. It would not be able to change its perspective of a problem such that it could resolve it. So what does it do then? It creates individuals. It's alike the reason we have genetic variations. We note no matter how intense a plague may be in a nation or people, there are always one or two people left standing, because in someway or other, their unique genetic structure has permitted them to survive or withstand its devastation. As long as we have a few of those survivors and as long as they can reproduce, the race continues on. But if the race all had exactly the same genetic structure, then a plague would wipe out the total race and the species would cease to exist.

The same principle operates in terms of differences in personality. We differ in personality ultimately because these differences contribute to the survival of the species. Hence our differences appear to maintain the whole. So the main problem of a society is to maintain enough cohesion so people can behave together and act in synchrony one with the other, cooperate with each other, but yet not be too rigidly organized so as to inhibit the creative perspectives of its individual members to problems and issues. This becomes the problem of society. Consequently there must always be that tension between being in the society, obeying its rules but being a little bit off, so that we can say, if we look at things this way maybe we work it out and thus we can deal with the situation effectively.

Psychosociohistory and Power as Cultural Creations

The personality itself must carry the element of society within itself. Most importantly, the thing we must note is that personality, consciousness and culture are *cultural* creations. The type of culture people exhibit, the type of consciousness we exhibit, the type of personality we exhibit, reflects the type of history and experience we have undergone as a people. When we let another people be the determiners of our history and experience, they then become the determiners of our consciousness, our personality and our culture.[23] Ultimately, we must recognize that we use consciousness to deal with the world. Culture is an adaptative tool; it's an instrument by which we deal with reality, by which we adapt to reality and by which we adapt reality to ourselves. The kind of consciousness we have will determine how we deal with reality. Consciousness, then, in the fact that it determines how we are going to deal with reality, how we change reality, *is* a power. Categorically, power is about enabling something to take place, the ability to do something, the ability to change something, the ability to adapt, the ability to defend one's self, the ability to change oneself in order to solve a problem. And therefore consciousness must be measured in terms of the degree to which it maintains our survival, advances our interests, puts us at the center of our concerns and at the center of our purposes. This is what culture connotes.

Culture: A Revolutionary Tool

Culture is not static. Culture is not stuck in one place. Culture itself must reconstruct itself if the system in which it exists is reconstructed and rearranged. Some of us get in trouble because we want to find an Afrikan culture stuck somewhere back in the thirteenth century and want to apply it to ourselves at this point in a different context. Afrikan culture is not a culture stuck in place and time. Afrikan culture is constantly changing and evolving because the context in which Afrikan people live changes and evolves. What makes it Afrikan culture is that it operates in the interest of Afrikan people, is designed to advance Afrikan people. When then we talk about Black culture, be sure we are not talking about a reactionary culture, a culture that has been generated in reaction to our abuse by white folks and to our control and domination by them. There's a large part of what we call Black culture that we need to exorcize from our psyches so that we can evolve an Afrikan-centered culture to advance our collective interests.[24]

Values as Directional Factors of Consciousness

Another very important aspect of consciousness is what we call *values*; those things that we prefer, those things that we see as right, those things that we think we should need, those things the pursuit of which determines our behavior and organizes our minds. Values are what I call the *directional factors* of consciousness. What are we talking about here? When you value something and that value is implanted in your brain, the brain calls forth all of its resources — all of its contents, the knowledge that it has available to it, the behavioral skills, the cognitive skills, the thinking skills and such things that it has available to it — organizes those things and relates them one to each other in such a way that the value can be achieved. When then we think about something we value and want to realize that something, we consciously or unconsciously assess our minds and ask: "Do I have the relevant knowledge? Do I have the relevant skills? Do I have the relevant thinking and cognitive skills so that I can organize this knowledge and skill in a way that can achieve those values?" If we believe we have those skills, if we believe we have the content, if we appropriately organize those contents through thought, then we pursue those values and chances and thus may realize those values. If though we have those values and we assess ourselves, we recognize that we don't have the appropriate skills, we don't have the appropriate knowledge and content, we don't have the appropriate thought styles and so forth, we then say, "Well, maybe we should develop the requisite skills, maybe we should learn the requisite knowledge, maybe we should develop the means of thinking." Once we do this we will then organize in a way to achieve our values.

Once we have values, are guided by values, and those values guide skills, content and so forth, we are empowered to realize those values. Therefore, values are a type of power. Where am I going with this? I am going with this to underscore that: If values are a type of power; if values are the things that guide our behavior; if culture is a type of power and consciousness is a type of power and personality is a type of power; if we let another people determine the nature of our consciousness, our personality and our values, they then gain power over us. If consciousness, culture, personality and values are instruments of power, they then use our consciousness, our values, our culture as *their* instruments of power .

How does this work in reality? They take our cultural products (our music, our song) and use them as their instruments of power and benefit from them.

Why Afrikan-centered Consciousness

What then is an Afrikan-centered consciousness? An Afrikan-centered consciousness is one that is based on Afrikan-centered content, Afrikan-centered knowledge, Afrikan-centered values, Afrikan-centered consciousness. To the degree that our consciousness is based on Afrikan-centered values and so forth, we are empowered as Afrikan people. To the degree those values and consciousness are determined by other people, we become their instruments of power and they use us against ourselves.

Consequently, if we are to be empowered and our power is to work in our interests, then our consciousness must be an Afrikan consciousness, our values must be Afrikan values, our personality must be an Afrikan-based personality. If not, we may suffer first *ethnocide* and then *genocide*. What we're saying here is that our culture will not be functional in a way that it protects our interests. We must then, as a people, develop a new Afrikan consciousness — an Afrikan-centered consciousness — and that means we develop it based on an Afrikan history, Afrikan culture and Afrikan values. *Most of all*, we must develop an Afrikan sense of nationhood.

The Need for Nation Consciousness and Vision

Many of the problems we suffer today are because we do not see ourselves as a nation. We complain about how we are segregated from everybody else, about how we are not a part of the mainstream, how we are not a part of the economy, how we are shut out from the government and the political process. If we are not a part of these things and yet these things are what define a nation, then we are *not* a part of the American nation: that nation is a *White* nation! We are in effect a *de facto* nation, but we are afraid to recognize it. If we looked at ourselves as a nation we'd see many of the reasons why we are where we are as a people. If we looked at ourselves as a nation, we would see why we have the problems we have. Why do we have some of the problems we have? For the same reason other Afrikan nations have the problems they have. Because we permit our resources, human and material, to be used by another people. We export them. We, like any other Afrikan nation, are an indebted nation; we are over-indebted. When talk about the Afrikan nation suffering from being overburdened by debt, we don't recognize that we are talking about ourselves. If I ask here tonight how many of us owe another black institution or another black person major debt, we would get very few hands. But if I ask how many of us owe a white person, a white institution, a non-Afrikan institution great debt, we'd all probably have to raise our hands. If you recognize this and add this up in terms of a nation, not just yourself as an individual but if you look at all of us individuals in terms of a nation, you will recognize that as a nation we owe an enormous debt to other people. One of the reasons why we are poverty-stricken is not because we don't have money; it's because all of our money is being used to service the debt that other nations own — that the White nation in America owns. Because we spend so much time paying our installment plans and paying our money out to these other nations of people, we cannot save our monies, we cannot accumulate our money and create wealth so that we can employ ourselves as a people, so that we can support our families as a people, so that we can build the schools we need to build to educate our children in the way we need to educate them as a people. Consequently we have the similar problem which all Afrikan nations have, almost where they cannot build highways, railways, schools, hospitals, institutions, communications and other systems because all of the wealth they are generating is being exported out to European nations and other nations to whom they owe debt. But you can only see this when you look at yourself as a nation. When you look at yourself as a nation you can see that you can change this problem by changing the debt relationship you have to other people.

Afrikan Nations as Monocultures

We shall talk about Afrikan nations as monocultures, meaning that they often exist by shipping out one or two major products (cocoa beans, oil, gold, bauxite etc.) into what we call a buyer's market. That is, the people to whom they sell these products set the prices they are going to pay for these products such that many of these nations are now being paid less for their products than they were being paid thirty years ago. Yet the nations that buy their products and lower the prices on their products are selling them back those products in processed form, selling them back their own products that have been manufactured here for higher and higher prices. Then we wonder why Afrika is in debt and impoverished. That's because they are caught up in an impoverishing mechanism. But we need not talk about the continental Afrikan, because we are in the same situation today.[25]

Afrikan American Nation as Monoculture

The Afrikan American nation is a monoculture. The commodity we sell is labor. We're not selling much manufacturing; we're not selling much other products. The major product we have to sell is the major commodity we were brought over here for in the first place — labor. Now we are selling our labor in a buyer's market, meaning that the people who buy our labor are buying it at the prices they set. And they keep devaluing the price they are willing to pay for our labor. On top of devaluing the price, they are no longer even demanding the labor. So after a while we won't be able to sell our labor at any price and we will then be totally deprived as a people.[26] Therefore, we are caught in a similar position. And just as there is social disorganization in the Afrikan nation, there is social disorganization in the Afrikan American nation. You cannot have your wealth flowing out of your nation; you cannot enrich other people at the expense of yourself and not have social disorganization.

Prescriptions for the Afrikan American Nation

If we look at ourselves as a nation, then the Afrikan American nation must do what all other nations do. We must capture our own internal resources; we must capture our own internal markets; we must trade within ourselves as a people and as a group and generate wealth within our own nation as a means of counterbalancing our dependence on Europeans and upon the white nation itself. In order to do this we must have a nation-consciousness; we must now organize and relate to it ourselves as a nation of people.

When we look at our relationship, say, to the Koreans as a nation, we see the same relationship Japan has to the United States of America as a nation. We notice that they are bargaining and negotiating trade agreements. Japan is building up its resources; it is blocking out U.S. industry from its nation, yet it is entering into the American markets and selling there and taking out the wealth from American markets. If we look at our relationship to Koreans, to Dominicans, to other groups, we will see the same relationships where those groups have entered into the Afrikan American nation, set up shop, and shipped out its wealth day-by-day and night-by-night. Yet the Afrikan American entrepreneurial nation is not permitted to set up shop in their midst, is not permitted to carry wealth from their nations. They then grow fat on the surplus they gain from the Afrikan American nation. This means then that if we think of ourselves as a nation we must protect our internal markets from the intrusion of outsiders. We must not permit them entry into our nation. As I look down 125th Street and see our people locked out on the outside, I agree with our vendors that if black men and black women cannot make a living on that street, then no other people should be permitted to make a living on that street. *We are not obligated in any kind of way to feed the children of other people before we feed our own!* But it's only if you think in terms of nationhood that you can resolve this kind of problem. We have tremendous possibilities as a black nation.

You can see these white boys over there pursuing China, don't you? They're in China knocking each other over trying to get to it. What is the China market worth to the European? The China market to the European is worth $500 billion at this point. Do you know what the Afrikan American market is worth to the European here in America? Over $400 billion. Our market is worth as much as the Chinese market, the Mexican market which they have drawn into NAFTA. It is worth more than the market of Canada. In other words, Afrikan American people have more to spend with this nation than does the nation of Canada. We have more to spend with this nation than many nations on this earth. Our population as a people is larger than many of the European nations and other nations on this earth. But because we are not organized as a nation, we do not force other people into NAFTA agreements with us. We are not able to place conditions on their entry into our market by saying, "If you enter here you are going to pay taxes; if you enter here you are going to leave something here; if you enter here you are going to leave money in these institutions; you are going to contribute to our schools; you are going to contribute to our recreational centers; you are going to contribute to the employment of our people and to the stability of our families. If you cannot contribute to these things, if you cannot contribute jobs, if you cannot contribute to the education of our people then we cannot permit you to operate within our borders. This is the way a nation runs.

You do not let another people walk in, have their way, walk out and leave you impoverished as a people in the name of "free markets." There's no such thing as a free and open market. That's white folk's propaganda! They *force* people into their markets. Fidel Castro was not free to say he won't be a part of it. When he refused to be a part of it they embargoed him, locked him out. The Japanese in the early part of the century said we don't want to be a part of your market. What did the United States do? They sent Admiral Perry in there and blasted those markets open. What free markets then? There are no such things as free markets and when you learn that you're going to be better for it.

We've got the markets but we are not taking advantage of it. We have gotten ourselves into a situation where we are locked out of other people's markets and we permit them into our own such that we are locked out of our own markets. Then we wonder why we suffer the way we do. It is not because we are poor. If we were that poor and impoverished then why did those people come to us to earn their living and earn their wealth? It means then we must be a wealthy people. We have as people everything that we need to make a nation. We have telephones, fax machines, computers, highways, bridges, railways, airways, waterways, trucks, everything that many nations in the world desire. In fact, the vast majority of nations wish they had available to them what the Afrikan American community has available to it. They wish they had the highways; they wish they had the trucks; they wish they had the trains, the ships, the computers, the telephones and equipment that you can just pick up and dial right away and don't have to be routed through France or somewhere else. They wish the electric lights didn't go off sporadically every day. They beg for consistency. We've got it all right here! Why then are we not better off than we are?

It is not enough to have gold in your soil, oil in your soil, diamonds in your soil; *you must have a consciousness.* It is only with an appropriate consciousness that these things can be transformed and converted into wealth and power and can be used for the advancement and survival of a people. The same is true here then. We cannot just have telephones, faxes, money in our pockets and such. That's not enough. We must have a consciousness that transforms those phones and those faxes into a communication network that unites a people across cities, regions, continents, and it becomes a basis for a system of distribution, a basis for creating and uniting a market from which one earns wealth that feeds one's family and thus stabilizes one's social situation. We can have all of these things, but if we don't have a sense of nation — if we do not have a group consciousness, if we do not identify ourselves as a nation — then these are but mere instruments. As a matter of fact, these become the means by which we destroy ourselves.

We are looking at the black buying power in the United States here 1990-95. We've got a report here called The Georgia Business and Economic Condition, published by the Selig Center of the University of Georgia[10] entitled "Black Buying Power by Place of Residence, 1990–1995, the second of a two-part analysis of buying power in specific markets. What are we talking about here? Was this published for us? No! It is published for white folks and it's telling them how much money black folks have. It's telling whites that the money black folks have is the difference between their success and their failure. It reads in part:

> Georgia's African American population thus controls approximately sixteen cents of each dollar in spending power. That is, about one dollar in six is spent by black consumers.[27]

How are we aware of the kind of power we have as Afrikan people? "Clearly, they are a substantial economic force throughout the state." But without a national consciousness we don't recognize that. However, whites recognize it. They go on to say:

> For many of Georgia's businesses the ability to capture black spending can make the difference between success and failure.[28]

They are putting it right in your face. If black spending power can make the difference between success and failure of Georgia's business — and we're talking about white folk's businesses — that means black folks have got Power,

10. This report is further dealt with in *Blueprint for Black Power* by the author.

because power is about the ability to succeed or to bring about failure. When somebody else's success or failure depends on your behavior then, you have power.

New York State is the largest black market in this country, the largest black market in the world. How much money are we worth in New York State, Black people? We are worth $61 billion. That is a lot of money. It represents well over 10 percent of the buying power in the New York/New Jersey/Connecticut area. What does that mean? But don't look at that absolute figure, look at what would happen if we reinvested that $61 billion; if we put that $61 billion in black businesses, in black trade, if we invested that $61 billion in gaining equity in the major American corporations, if we used that $61 billion to gain equity in Afrikan countries. I was reading a piece this week about the fact that a couple of black investment bankers are selling as much $100 million of bonds for the African Development Bank. Another black investment banker is selling something like $500 million of securities for Afrikan businesses and infra-structural development. What does that mean, Afrikan people? That means that if we were knowledgeable of corporate finance, if we were knowledgeable of investment vehicles, we could literally finance the development of Afrika by buying securities in the Afrikan Development Bank, by buying bonds and buying over investment instruments in Afrikan corporations — even if they are owned by white folks — because once we buy the shares we become the owners. In other words, by using black wealth we can become the vehicle for financing Afrikan growth and development. By using our own wealth and financing our own businesses, developing our own economic systems, we would multiply our wealth and we would not only be worth $400 billion but we'd be worth $800 billion or more and growing stronger. The stronger we grow the more others would depend upon how we spend in order to survive and to that degree we will gain power over them. What if tomorrow we decided, as Afrikan people, to build coop supermarkets across this country so that we could sell our people groceries and food below wholesale prices? If we decided, using our church organizations as a means for sponsoring these co-op food markets across the country, we can open them literally simultaneously and center then the buying power for all of those co-op centers in a way that we would have billions of dollars to spend with the suppliers of food. We could then manipulate those producers in terms of the buying power we have. We could begin then to place our people on their boards; we could begin then to have real and substantial power in America. We have it in our hands, but we've got to think in terms of nation.

It becomes interesting when you study this particular breakdown of black spending in Georgia. I wish we would get these breakdowns across the country. When you become a state and a nation you develop *state*-istics; that's where statistics come from. It is the means by which a state and a nation gathers information about itself so that it can use that information to reorganize itself and to set itself up in ways to advance its interests. Once you become a nation, you become sensitive to the fact that you need a lot of information so that you can use this information. When I read about the percentage of black buying power in Georgia by county, something becomes very surprising. You note, for instance, that black buying power is as high as 25 percent and 26 percent in many of these counties. For example, in Liberty County, Georgia, black buying power there is 22 percent of the total buying power. In Merthwether, 25 percent; Peach County, 25 percent. In some of these black counties, black buying power is as much as 45 percent. In other words, the black consumer has these counties by the neck. They are able, if that buying power was to be coordinated and used, to have real impact and to transform the power relations of those societies and of those counties. They would be able, if they are buying half, 25 percent or 30 percent of what is being bought in those counties, to establish their own businesses and enterprises there and they would be able to defend those business enterprises through the use of the boycott weapon.

What we are saying here unequivocally this evening, Brothers and Sisters, is that Afrikan power is based on an Afrikan consciousness, based on an Afrikan-centered culture, based on an Afrikan-centered personality. The degree to which our personalities and our culture are based on Afrikan values, based on Afrikan interests and based on Afrikan goals, to that degree we empower ourselves as Afrikans and to that degree we escape the power of others over us.

Thank you very much.

Endnotes

1. Duff, Christina. "Redefining the Good Life: Indulging in Inconspicuous Consumption." *Wall Street Journal*. 4/14/1997. p. B1.

Robin, Vicki. "Poor Nations Call Our Bluff on Consumption." *New York Newsday*. 10/31/1994. p. A27.

2. Mosle, Sara. "Scores Count. Principal Michael Johnson is helping poor black students pass state exams. So why do school reformers see him as a pariah." *New York Times Magazine*. 9/8/1996. p. 41.

Sengupta, Somini. "At Oasis of Achievement, Principal Fights for Job." *New York Times*. 01/29/1997. p. B9.

3."When you realize how unworthy your master is, you'll no longer serve him." — Prof. John Henrik Clarke

4. French, Howard W. "The Great Gold Rush in Zaire. Mining Concerns Court Rebels Even Before Mobutu's Ouster." *The New York Times*. April 18, 1997. p. A6.

Bonner, Raymond. "Westerners Angle for Mining Stakes in Congo." *The New York Times*. June 17, 1997. p. D4.

5. Hosokawa, Bill. 1969. *Nisei: The Quiet Americans*. New York: William Morrow.

Wilson, Robert A. and Hosokawa, Bill. 1982. *East to America: A History of the Japanese in the United States*. New York: Quill/William Morrow.

Takaki, Ronald. 1993. *A Different Mirror: A History of Multicultural America*. Boston/Toronto/London: Little, Brown & Company.

6. Connors, Cathy. 1994. "Harlem Hosts Clintons: President Visits Historic Church; Preaches 'Sermon.' *New York Amsterdam News*. Vol. 85, No. 40. p. 1.

7. Robin, Vicki. "Poor Nations Call Our Bluff on Consumption." *New York Newsday*. October 31, 1994. p. A27.

8. "Power is the ability to define reality and to have others respond to it as their reality." — Dr. WADE NOBLES

9. Bloomfield, Maxwell. *Dixon's The Leopard's Spots: A Study in Popular Racism* in *White Racism: Its History, Pathology and Practice.* Barry N. Schwartz & Robert Disch (eds.) New York: Dell, 1970, p. 111.

10. Good God who created the Sun which shines on us from above, who rouses the sea and makes the thunder rumble: Listen! God though hidden in a cloud watches over us. The god of the white man calls forth crime but our God wills good works. Our God who is so good commands us to vengeance. He will direct our arms and help us. Throw away the likeness of the white man's god who has so often brought us to tears and listen to liberty which speaks in all our hearts.

— BOUKMAN August 22, 1791.

Jacob H. Carruthers, *The Irritated Genie: An Essay on the Haitian Revolution.* Chicago: The Kemetic Institute,1985, p. 22.

"We will be well on our way as a people when an Afrikan leader will boldly and unapologetically pray to an Afrikan god in public."

— Dr. J.H. CLARKE

Welsing, Dr. Frances Cress. 1980. "The Concept of the Color of God and Black Mental Health." *Black Books Bulletin.* Chicago: Institute of Positive Education, pp. 27-35.

Bishop Henry McNeal Turner. 1898. "God Is A Negro," reprinted in *Black Nationalism in America.* Eds. John H. Bracey, Jr., August Meier and Elliot Rudwick. Indianapolis: Bobbs-Merrill Educational Publishing, 1970, pp. 154-155.

"Black Experience of Religion must obviously consider the black man within the context of the traditional religion of his Afrikan forefathers, the integrity both of the black man as well as of Africa being maintained. Most of us know only too well that such terms like "Afrikan Traditional Religion" are often used to identify an ersatz system assembled from the questionable findings of even more questionable authorities, and that a great show of seriously considering this perversion is made, while in face it is being used as a foil to highlight the virtues of "Christianity" or "Islam" over all traditional beliefs of Africa."

— FELA SOWANDE. 1970. *Black Experience of Religion.* Washington, DC: Howard University Press, p. 4.

11. Wright, Dr. Bobby E. 1985. "Black Suicide: Lynching by Any Other Name Is Still Lynching." *The Psychopathic Racial Personality and Other Essays.* Chicago: Third World Press, pp. 16-22.

12. "Every day of our lives we are in the front ranks of battle."

— HENRY DAVID THOREAU

"We need to take inventory every night and see how much of us is left at the end of the day." — MAULANA KARENGA

13. Goleman, Daniel. "Probing the Enigma of the Multiple Personality," *New York Times*, Science Times, June 28, 1988.

14. Ibid.

15. Wilson, Amos N. 1993. "European Historiography and Oppression Exposed: An Afrikan Analysis and Perspective"in *The Falsification of Afrikan Consciousness*. New York: Afrikan World InfoSystems.

16. *New York Times*, Science Times, June 28, 1988.

17. Ibid.

18. Malcolm X used to say that if your religion has not done anything more for than it already has [based on the current condition of our people] then you need to get rid of it.

19. *New York Times*, Science Times, June 28, 1988.

20. Aesop's Fables: The Story of the Four Bulls standing back to back as a demonstration of unity as strength in a victorious battle against the lion. Individually each would have been consumed.

"He must first have sacrificed his individuality at the altar of what Jung terms "individuation," through which "he becomes not only an individual but also a member of a collectivity, and the wholeness he has achieved is in contact, through consciousness and the unconscious, with the whole world. The accent is not on his supposed individuality as opposed to his collective obligations, but ... on the fulfillment of his own nature as it is related to the whole." How he does this, he must find out, for he is his own initiator; no one can help him; no one can filch from him the peace which passeth understanding that comes with achievement. But he will not travel in an air-conditioned car on tarred roads; it is not a journey to be undertaken, and perhaps only a sense of compulsion that drives one on regardless of aught else will ensure success."

—FELA SOWANDE. 1967. "The Development of a National Tradition of Music." *Aspects of Nigerian Music*, pp. 54-55.

21. Religion is the inner awareness of a factual dynamic relationship between the individual on one hand and the Cosmos and the World of Nature on the other.

Philosophy is the articulation of that relationship in a meaningful intelligible way, as a guide to practical living.

Drama is the enactment of that relationship, in movement and speech.

Art is the meaningful expression of that relationship in any medium whatever.

History is the factual record of that relationship in its process of becoming; not as mere statistical facts, but as the detailed diary of the contacts between Man, Cosmos and Nature, from which were eventually distilled that clear awareness of the interdependence and the unbroken continuity between the three worlds.

The science of social organization is an accurate reproduction of that same relationship, in terms of human society.

The science of government is the codification of that relationship and its application of that society, its purpose being to subserve the science of social organization.

Economics, Family structure, and the Individual within the Family, are determined by, and subserve, the science of government and the science of social organization.

—FELA SOWANDE "Black Folklore." *Black Lines,* Fall 1971. Pittsburgh, PA: University of Pittsburgh, Black Studies Dept., pp. 21-22.

22. It is the LIVINGNESS in Art that makes it art. Form, style, structure, craftsmanship, are of the highest degree of importance to the creative mind in man, for meaningful ideas have nothing to say to the man who has not mastered the tools of his trade. Nevertheless it is only when even superb craftsmanship has been successfully wedded to—and has become a channel for—a "Poetic Content" that adds new dimensions and insight, greater depth and clarity, to man's awareness and understanding of himself in relation to a dynamic Universe of which is an integral and indispensable unit, that we have Art in which there is that Livingness that makes it art. Only in terms of that "Poetic Content" can that Art be profitably approached, examined, and appraised. Only by being in the final analysis primarily concerned, not with the formal and structural elements, but with the LIFE-QUALITY in that Art can one be certain that he is handling the Art itself and not its mere container.

— FELA SOWANDE. 1969. *The Role of Music in African Society.* Washington, DC: Howard University Press, p. 20.

"Now if you want to study religion, you'll have to find out what the elements are. There are three elements in religion: symbols, myths and rites. Symbols are tokens, things that stand for something else. And in the Ancient Egyptian Mysteries, the symbols were the things that were shown, the myths were the things that were told and the rites were the things that were performed or acted. You take these three elements and you have the mysteries, which were the secret rites of the Ancient Egyptians [Kemites]."

– JOHN G. JACKSON. "Christianity Before Christ." A lecture delivered on May 16, 1981 at the First World Alliance, Harlem, NY.

– JOHN G. JACKSON. 1971. *The Mysteries of Egypt.* Chicago: MASS Inc.

23. "History is a clock that people use to tell their time of day and it is the compass that people use to locate themselves on the map of human geography. It tells you where you've been, what you are, and where you are. But most important, history tells where you still must go and what you still must be." – Prof. JOHN HENRIK CLARKE

24. Karenga, Maulana. 1980. *Kawaida Theory: An Introductory Outline.* Inglewood, CA: Kawaida Publications.

25. Rodney, Walter. 1974. *How Europe Underdeveloped Africa.* Washington, DC: Howard University Press.

26. When the Agriculture Revolution ended and the Industrial Revolution started the capitalists found that Chattel Slavery didn't produce much of a profit. In order for the capitalists to keep anything it has to pay a profit. So they got rid of Chattel Slavery and they took these so-called Chattel slaves and told them, "Now you're ex-slaves; you're free." They switched us over from Chattel Slavery to Wage Slavery.

Now machines are doing all the work so they don't need Wage slaves, so we are Welfare slaves now. I told the young lady that the capitalists don't need our labor anymore the next thing they might do is to commit genocide. In other words, they don't need these people anymore so they'll put us behind barb wire, set up the gas ovens and exterminate us. I think that's the way the world is going unless we can do something about it.

–JOHN G. JACKSON "Christianity Before Christ." Lecture of May 16, 1981 at the First World Alliance, Harlem, New York.

27. "Black Buying Power By Place of Residence, 1990–1995; the Second of a Two Part Analysis of Buying Power in Specific Markets." *Georgia Business and Economic Condition.* Athens, GA: Selig Center of the University of Georgia.

28. Ibid.

These notes were compiled by ADISA MAKALANI, an affiliated editor. We thought they would complement this publication.

Index

Study Materials and Book Promotion Ads

Books by Afrikan World InfoSystems

Black-on-Black Violence:
The Psychodynamics of Black Self-Annihilation in Service of White Domination

A piercing insight into the nature and causes of Black-on-Black violence.
Third Edition

ISBN 978-1-879164-00-0
PB. Pages: 236
$21.00

The Developmental Psychology of the Black Child
Second Edition

The best selling text on Black child development.

ISBN 978-1-879164-13-2
PB. Pages: 320
$22.00

Awakening the Natural Genius of Black Children
Fourth Edition

In this insightful text Dr. Wilson asserts, "Black children have a natural head start," and sets out to prove it.

ISBN 978-1-879164-01-7
PB. Pages: 192
$18.00

Afrikan-Centered Consciousness Versus The New World Order: Garveyism in the Age of Globalism
(illustrated with maps)

A splendid introductory text on the survival of Afrikan Nationalism in the face of the new imperialism.

ISBN 978-1-879164-09-4
PB. Pages: 160
$18.00

Books by Afrikan World InfoSystems

Blueprint For Black Power: A Moral, Political and Economic Imperative for the Twenty-First Century

Masterful, nothing less than brilliant!

ISBN 978-1-879164-06-2
PB. pages: 912
$52.00

ISBN 978-1-879164-07-9
HC. Pages: 912
$90.00

Issues of Manhood in Black and White: An Imcisive Look into Masculinity and the Societal Definition of Afrikan Man

A ground-breaking text, a leader in its field!

ISBN 978-1-879164-14-7
PB. Pages: 184
$18.00

Distorted Truths: The Bastardization of Afrikan Cosmology
S. K. Damani Agyekum

A forceful and intelligent approach exposing Western bastardization of Afrikan Cosmology throughout history.

ISBN 978-879164-12-3
PB. Pages: 512
$32.00

The Falsification of Afrikan Consciousness: Eurocentric History, Psychiatry and the Politics of White Supremacy

A multi part series that boldly challenges entrenched Eurocentric institutions.

ISBN 978-1-879164-02-7
PB. Pages: 160
$18.00

Profiles of Acclaimed Books by AWIS

Blueprint For Black Power: *A Moral, Economic and Political Imperative for the 21st Century* details a master plan for the power revolution necessary for Black survival in the 21st century. It illuminates that though Afrikan Americans take home nearly $500 billion yearly of the trillions they generate, they retain a mere 5% of this income. Viewed as a nation their economy would be 8th or 9th largest in the world! Wilson argues that were it to view itself a *de facto* nation and organize as such, then its incessant scourge of poverty, crime, dis-employment, mis-education, mis-leadership, consumerism and powerlessness would be drastically reduced. He deconstructs and delegitimates the U.S. governmental, corporate and power-elite structures, debunks ethnocentrism, global imperial capitalism and their portent for Afrikan communities locally and peoples globally. Furthermore, he roundly castigates the ineptitude of Black sycophantic religious/political leadership.

Blueprint warns of Black obsolescence in the coming millennia! It mandates and instructs searing, radical approaches and opportunities for true global Black Power.
✦ Available in Library HB/PB. PAGES: 912

The Developmental Psychology of the Black Child, 2ND EDITION.

- Are Black and White children the same?
- Is the Black child a White child who happens to be "painted" Black?
- Are there any significant differences in the mental and physical development of Black and White children?
- Do Black parents socialize their children to be inferior to White children?

This pioneering book looks at these and other related controversial questions from an Afrikan perspective. The topics of growth, development and education are scholarly explored.

Expanded, updated, indexed, this text was fortified with new foreword, charts, and user-friendly typeset. PB. PAGES: 320

Afrikan-Centered Consciousness versus the New World Order: *Garveyism in the Age of Globalism* consists of two spellbinding lectures buttressed by a scintillating overview. This modest text challenges the all too pervasive assumption and false perception that the "New World Order" is somehow ordained; that if Afrikan people are to progress, they have no other alternative but to remain colonized by white Western interests. This of course is patently false. Dr. Wilson debunks this myth with an insightful analysis of the Legacy of Marcus Garvey and the proven validity of Afrikan-centered consciousness as necessary psychological and material tools in the struggle for advancement and true liberation.

Wilson puts forth his argument in ways that grab the general reader and simultaneously reduces the much-touted strategic thinking of the proponents of the New World Order to the mere newspeak it really is. With its exceptional charts and brilliant analysis of black thought, this text has become the perfect primer and complement to *Blueprint For Black Power* published one year prior. PB. PAGES: 160

Black-on-Black Violence: *The Psychodynamics of Black Self-Annihilation in Service of White Domination* represents a distinct milestone in criminology and Afrikana Studies. Its explanatory perspectives are exceptionally insightful and iconoclastic. Its main thesis is that the operational existence of *Black-on--Black* violence in the United States is psychologically and economically mandated by the White American-dominated status quo. The criminalization of the Black American male is a psychopolitically engineered process geared to maintain dependency and relative powerlessness of the Afrikan American and Pan-Afrikan communities. Wilson exposes the psychosocial and intrapsychical dynamics of *Black-on-Black* criminality and lays the intellectual foundation for its social eradication. PB. Pages: 232

Issues of Manhood in Black and White: *An Incisive Look into Masculinity and the Societal Definition of Afrikan Man,* explores the age-old issue of "what is a man," "be a man," man as leader, provider and producer—issues encased in a political, economic, social and geopolitical frame-work largely in the manufacture and control of a dominating power oft-times white, racist, ruthless, American—where ambition and opportunities to succeed are curtailed, few, education poor or inappropriate, history and psychohistory deemed irrelevant. Wilson takes this issue by the scruff in his accustomed way, rendering a searingly absolutely brilliant treatise for any historical time, *particularly now,* in view of the right wing ascent to government nationwide.

In Part II, *Understanding Black Adolescent Male Violence,* Wilson shows in brilliant detail how American society creates and sustains Black adolescent criminality in its inner-cities across the U.S.; that Black-on-Black adolescent violence is rooted in historical and contemporary White-on-Black violence. Wilson, as such, advances a continental Afrikan paradigm worthy of discussion and applicability to Diasporan males. PB. PAGES. 184

The Falsification of Afrikan Consciousness: *Eurocentric History, Psychiatry and the Politics of White Supremacy* is a triple feature. Part I, *Eurocentric Historiography in the European Oppression of Afrikan People* was among the first contemporary analyses delineating the role that Eurocentric history-writing plays in rationalizing European oppression of Afrikan peoples and in falsifying Afrikan consciousness. It explicates why we should study history; how history-writing shapes the psychology of peoples and individuals; how this history as mythology creates, in Afrikans, historical amnesia that robs their material, mental, social and spiritual wherewithal for overcoming poverty and oppression.

Part II, *Eurocentric Political Dogmatism,* contends that the alleged mental and behavioral maladaptiveness of oppressed Afrikan peoples is a political-economic necessity for the maintenance of White domination and imperialism. It indicts the Eurocentric mental health establishment for entering into collusion with the Eurocentric political establishment to egregiously oppress and exploit Afrikan peoples by misdiagnosing, mislabeling and mistreating reactions to oppression. PB. PAGES: 160

Awakening the Natural Genius of Black Children. Afrikan children are naturally precocious and gifted. They begin life with a "natural head start." Intelligence is not fixed at birth. There is clear evidence that the quality of children's educational experiences during infancy and early childhood are substantially related to their measured intelligence, academic achieve-ment and social behavior. Wilson reveals the daily routines, child-rearing practices, parent-child interactions, games and play materials, parent training and pre-school programs which have made demonstrably outstanding and lasting differences in the intellectual, academic and social performance of Afrikan American children. Updated with a new foreword this text remains a tour de force. PB. Pages: 192

Distorted Truths: *The Bastardization of Afrikan Cosmology* deconstrcts Western thought and Judaeo-Christian practice by exposing their theft, outright bastardization and usurpation of Afrikan cosmology and history. It reframes Diop's *Civilization or Barbarism* and George James' *Stolen Legacy* unveiling Western scholars fraudulent search for white supremacy, their obfuscation of Afrika's origin and contribution to world culture and civilization.

It retraces Grimaldi out-migrations from Afrika into Europe and beyond. He profiles the Dogon, Bambara, Mbuti, Twa, San, and Khoi as existing cosmological systems.

Aptly illustrated, Agyekum courses us through astronomy, archeology, paleontology, anthropology, Nile Valley history, Greece, Rome, Byzantium, early Christianity and related disciplines. P.B. PAGES: 512

The Psychology of Self-Hatred and Self-Defeat: Towards a Reclamation of the Afrikan Mind
Author: Amos N. Wilson
Editor: S.N. Plata

A splendid work of candor, finest articulation, penetrating insights and prescriptions
First Edition

ISBN 978-1-879164-15-4
PB. Pages: 344
$29.00

- Why was it necessary that self-hatred be "created" in the black body?
- Why are negative assignations applied to black and blackness as were expressed in the Oxford English dictionary of the 16th Century?
- Why was black *degraded* and allied to Satan, evil, moral or physical dirtiness, obeah, sin, death, war, famine and all forms of omen, badness, and dread?
- How has induced slave mentality been made to play itself out in our current behavior?
- Why must the Afrikan be educated into ignorance; is education a type of conditioning?
- Is the Black college necessary now that we've been admitted to white schools?
- The European college is a part of European self-defense. Conversely, why then are Black Studies being throttled, marginalized, electived — not mandated?
- Can the experience of slavery be seen as just an exploitation of our bodies, a period of brainwashing, even more so a period of character creation?
- Why do the oppressed react to frustration with apathy, anger, regression, denial, color-blindness, reality distortion, narcissism, falsified consciousness, false morality, "acting white," intellectualization, and phantasmic identification with the oppressor?
- Why are we praying to the same god white people are praying to yet get the bad end of the stick while whites get the good end repeatedly?
- Blacks and whites with the same values, does believing "thou shalt not steal"—even what they stole from us—keep us impoverished and instead protect their wealth?
- Why is Science just as much a political product as is Sociology and Psychology?
- What inferential abilities must blacks acquire to overcome white supremacy?
- Are significant numbers of black people addicted to white people, delusional that if white-folk would accept us, love, treat us like they treat themselves, wouldn't it be wonderful and we'd be *free at last* and with them live *happily ever after?*

For 20 hours, Wilson lays bare these questions. A sound analysis has inbuilt its own suggested solutions. Indeed, Wilson tasks himself its reveal by proffering *inferences* and *choices* rarely seen. This is a mandatorily interrogative exposition — a riveting read.

Dr. Amos N. Wilson 1941-1995

About the Author

Professor Amos N. Wilson is a former social caseworker, supervising probation officer, psychological counselor, training administrator in New York City Department of Juvenile Justice, and Assistant Professor of Psychology at the City University of New York.

Born in Hattiesburg, Mississippi, in 1941, Amos Nelson Wilson completed his undergraduate degree at the acclaimed Morehouse College in Atlanta, Georgia. He later migrated to New York where he mastered at The New School For Social Research before attaining his doctorate from Fordham University, New York City, in the field of General Theoretical Psychology.

Familiarly referred to as Brother Amos, he availed himself for numerous appearances at educational, cultural and political organizations such as the First World Alliance, the Afrikan Poetry Theatre, Afrikan Echoes, House of Our Lord Church, the Patrice Lumumba Coalition, the Slave Theatre, and CEMOTAP, to name just a few. His travels took him throughout the United States, to Canada and the Caribbean. Dr. Wilson's activities transcended academia into the field of business, owning and operating various enterprises in the greater New York area.

A prolific writer, Wilson has penned other pertinent works in the areas of education, child development and therapeutic psychology which we hope to share with our readers in the near future.

AWIS Authorized/Authentic AUDIO MP3 CDs by AMOS WILSON

Lecture Titles	CATALOG NUMBER	PRICE
The Third Reconstruction: Moving Beyond Civil and Human Rights into Afrikan Revolution *plus bonus* Who Will Bell the Cat?...	MP911502	$15.00
Who Will Bell the Cat? *De*-constructing the U.S. Violence Initiative	MP921809	$ 8.00
Tools of Empire: Construction, Destruction, and Reconstruction of Afrikan Civilizations 3500BCE to 2100AD	MP199102	$15.00
Black-on-Black Violence: White-engineered Self-annihilation in the Black Community	MP912402	$15.00
Culture and Identity: Critical Analyses and Pragmatic Approaches to Feel-good History and Conspiracy Theories	MP932401	$15.00
European Historiography and Oppression Exposed: An Afrikan Analysis	MP890205	$15.00
Death at an Early Age: The Failure of the American Education System	MP199906	$15.00
Effectuating an Afrikan Revolutionary Psychotherapy	MP840124	$15.00
Afrikan-centered Consciousness, Personality and Culture as Instruments of Power (misnomered Blueprint for Black Power)	MP942109	$15.00
European Psychological Warfare Against Afrikans	MP891502	$15.00
The Psychology of Cooperative Economics in the Black Community	MP200006	$15.00
The Crisis of Leadership in the Black Community	MP000000	$15.00
Issues of Manhood in Black and White	MP901125	$15.00
Developing an Afrikan Psychology of Liberation	MP852212	$15.00
Awakening the Natural Genius of Black Children	MP930393	$15.00
Riot or Revolt: The LA Rebellion and Urban Responses to State Injustice and Brutality	MP920601	$15.00
Special Education: Its Special Agenda Unhooded	MP930108	$15.00
The Legacy of Marcus Garvey: The True vs False/Pseudo Nationalist	MP870125	$15.00
The Economic Psychology of Afrikan Nationalism	MP872501	$15.00
The Falsification of Afrikan Consciousness	MP933010	$15.00
Black Male Female Relationships: Searing Perspectives	MP911124	$15.00
Eurocentric Political Dogmatism: Mental Health Mis-Diagnosis of Afrikan People	MP851801	$15.00
Rethinking Education: Star Wars and Millennia Beyond	MP1980XX	$15.00
Black Entertainment White Profits: An Outrage	MP940716	$15.00
The Importance and Challenge of Afrikan Parenting	MP872011	$15.00

Shipping & Handling 1-2 CD Sets $4.95 3-5 CD Sets $6.95 ✱ Call about DVDs

• **Note:** Prices are subject to change without notice. **Tel. 718 462-1830**